Dona Z. Meilach

CREATIVE CARVING

materials, techniques, appreciation

PITMAN PUBLISHING

FIRST PUBLISHED IN GREAT BRITAIN 1971

SIR ISAAC PITMAN AND SONS LTD.
Pitman House, Parker Street, Kingsway, London, W.C.2B 5PB
P.O. Box 6038, Portal Street, Nairobi, Kenya

SIR ISAAC PITMAN (AUST.) PTY. LTD.
Pitman House, Bouverie Street, Carlton, Victoria 3053, Australia

PITMAN PUBLISHING COMPANY S.A. LTD.
P.O. Box 9898, Johannesburg, S. Africa

For Melvin Meyer Meilach

Foreword

Anyone who has ever cut a shape from a sheet of paper has, in essence, carved. He has visualized a form within the blank rectangular sheet and released that form by cutting away the unessential part. Carving for sculpture involves the same problem of visualizing a shape within a block of wood, of stone, of soap or other material and then subtracting the unessential material to release that shape. Working with a three-dimensional block is more difficult than cutting a flat figure from a sheet of paper, but it is extremely challenging and satisfying.

Although carving is an ancient technique, this book illustrates that innovations in materials and methods are constantly evolving. Often traditional methods are used with new materials, new methods are used with traditional materials. The results reflect the latest artistic thinking.

The examples in this book are planned so the beginner may work with inexpensive, easy-to-carve soft materials and then progress to the harder materials. But he should feel free to skip around the book, selecting any material for a beginning that is available and appeals to him. There are no patterns to follow that will guarantee a successful first attempt. The examples offered represent artistic statements that are the result of grappling with the problems inherent to the art form and the media.

It is virtually impossible for any one person to be proficient in all techniques. For each chapter, many artists were consulted and their work photographed. The book is the result of observations, interviews and correspondence with artists in several countries and throughout the United States.. It is also a comprehensive guide to the materials and tools available for carving today.

The student, teacher and professional artist, the hobbyist and craftsman who use this book should remember that none of the techniques are absolute. They may be modified. There may be scores of ways to approach sculpture by carving. The methods shown are meant to open your eyes and mind to the approach of others, as if you were in the artists' studios observing them at work. Let these examples stimulate your thinking.

Acknowledgments

The artists, art students and craftsmen whose work is shown in these pages are the real creators of this book. All who have shared their ideas and their examples have my deepest gratitude. Their names appear with their work.

I wish also to thank the schools and teachers who cooperated by having their students develop art work using many of the materials discussed in this book. The Institute of Design, of the Illinois Institute of Technology (I.I.T.), permitted me to photograph its students at work, and their critiques. Mr. Dennis J. Kowal, Jr., of the Art Department, University of Illinois, Champaign-Urbana, was extremely cooperative. Mr. A. S. Bisock and Mr. Stanley Filar of the Chicago School of Art and Design, Ltd., welcomed me to the classroom. Miss Lorna Neubacher of the Ravenna High School, Ravenna, Ohio, had her students develop carvings from plaster blocks for this book. Mr. Egon Weiner of the Art Institute of Chicago demonstrated stone carving techniques.

My sincere appreciation to the galleries, museums and art groups who have loaned me photos from their collections and permitted me to come into their rooms to take my own pictures.

The executives of the sculpture and industrial firms I contacted for information about their products and services were extremely cooperative. They provided samples of the product, which I was able to test and photograph in use. Some were able to provide photographs of their product as finished art.

I am also indebted to Mr. Ben Lavitt and Mr. Harold Smolar, Astra Photo, Inc., Chicago, who worked closely with me to assure the best possible prints from photographs often taken under less than ideal lighting conditions.

I could never adequately express my indebtedness to my husband, Dr. Melvin Meilach, who assisted me in my search for and discovery of the artists whose work best illustrates the principles of the book. He has helped with the photography at more art fairs, art exhibits, art studios, museums and galleries than I have the energy to remember.

Dona Z. Meilach
Chicago, Illinois

Note: Photographs by the author unless otherwise credited.

Contents

CREATIVE CARVING

Composition, Henry Moore. Green Hornton stone. COLLECTION, MRS. IRWINA MOORE. COURTESY, ARTIST

1 About Carving

Carving is as old as civilization; it is as modern as tomorrow. Ancient man carved lines in his cave dwellings and shaped pebbles to represent magical and sacred images. Man has always carved stone, marble, bone, horn and other materials for symbolic, decorative and expressive purposes. After the seventeenth century, carved sculptures were most often made by the artist as a plaster or clay model. Then, with the use of a pointing machine—a simple instrument for measuring exactly a three-dimensional object—his model was reproduced in stone by highly skilled craftsmen. Sculptures produced in this way have slick, polished surfaces and highly realistic, unexpressive forms that make them appear lifeless and static to us today.

When twentieth-century artists rediscovered the satisfaction of working directly with their carving materials, it had a far-reaching impact on modern sculpture.

The nineteenth-century French sculptor Auguste Rodin made the first break. Although he had craftsmen carve the final sculpture, he supervised the production closely, dictating where specific areas were to remain roughcut and textured. Gauguin, early in the 1900's, emphasized the necessity of the artist's physical involvement with his materials. He worked directly with ceramics and wood, as a carver, familiarizing himself with and feeling a part of his materials. About the same time, African tribal carvings were brought to the Western World and artists found their simplicity refreshing, inspiring. Brancusi and other sculptors turned back to wood and stone; slowly but surely they learned to use the chisel and hammer themselves.

Today's carvers, such as Henry Moore and Barbara Hepworth, continue to discover new forms uniquely expressive of the time. They explore and exploit new materials to use with old tools, and new tools to use with traditional and modern materials. They are immensely sensitive to their materials, truthful to them and skillful in handling them.

Carving is a sculptural art because it exists in three dimensions. Carved sculpture may be of three types: (1) *in the round*, where the figure may be seen from all sides; (2) *relief*, where the figure stands away from the background; and (3) *intaglio*, where the figure is incised below the background.

Carving is a "subtractive" art because one must remove or subtract material to reach the final form. To create a sculpture from a log, wood must be subtracted or carved away. "I mean by sculpture," said Michelangelo, "that which is done by taking off." He spoke of releasing an image that he envisaged imprisoned in the block of wood or stone.

The opposite of carving is modeling where a material is "added" to build up a form. The modeler adds or builds up clay over an armature to create a sculpture.

Devoting an entire book to the carving method does not cast a ballot in favor of one technique over another; it simply means there are so many materials, methods and forms of expression used by the carver that a penetrating survey of contemporary activity yields new ideas for sculptors, teachers and students.

If you visualize the materials of the carver as only those for working stone and marble, you may think carving is an exceptionally difficult art form. It need not be, because there are many materials other than stone to carve, materials that are soft and relatively permanent. The beginning carver finds that he can experiment with three-dimensional concepts of volume and mass in space by working with wood, wax, plastic, soapstone and various other mineral and man-made materials now available. He will discover that industrial tools such as pneumatic drills, power saws, sanders and polishers greatly simplify the mechanics of carving. A sculptor may block out a shape from a log with a chain saw in an hour or so; the same results would take three or four days with an axe.

Artists differ in their approach to carving, of course. Some develop forms because they have certain tools and materials available, with which they have become familiar. This availability may dictate—and sometimes limit—artistic expression.

Other artists will visualize a form and then seek the best materials for realizing it. They experiment, innovate—and often are led in this way into new areas.

One sculptor may make definitive drawings for each surface to be carved; he may work from clay or plaster models and then attempt to duplicate them. Another may carve spontaneously, with only a mental image of what he hopes to release from the materials.

This illustrates an essential point: *there is no one best way to approach carving or any act of creative expression.* If there were, everyone would produce carbon copies of one another's work. The methods and media shown are enormously important; but they are, ultimately, only the means to communicate an endless variety of thoughts and emotions.

The chapters are arranged so you may begin with materials and tools you may have and that are easy to work with. Whether you are carving for the first or the hundredth time, the examples are offered, not to be imitated, but to stimulate individual artistic expression.

gyptian Stone Relief. Section of west wall, Tomb of Unisankh, early 6th Dynasty. Carvings portray scenes from the life the person buried in the tomb. COURTESY, FIELD MUSEUM OF NATURAL HISTORY, CHICAGO

Carvings can be simple geometric shapes repeated in a variety of materials. Here, the sphere shape is interpreted differently in plastic and wood by a student of the Institute of Design, I. I. T., Chicago.

A very intricate carving using a full ivory elephant tusk. COLLECTION, DR. JOEL D. ARNOLD, OAK PARK, ILLINOIS

Subjects for Carved Sculpture

The artist always has been involved with his environment and culture. This involvement is reflected in his art. Today's themes often have scientific and mechanical connotations, because these are part of the artist's environment and concerns.

The subject for a sculpture is highly individualistic, yet it will probably fall into the categories of a human or animal shape, an organic form derived from nature, or a man-made object. Ideas may be realistic, stylized or abstract. They may be symbolic of love, death, or some deep emotional vision of the artist. They may be created simply to take advantage of the inherent texture and color of a material.

Rarely do ideas spring full-blown from one source; more often they are a composite of mental impressions the artist has stored up as a result of training his eye to constantly search for sources for sculptural form, and of reacting to them. An abstract form may be based on cloud formations, a mound of sand, the bend in a leaf. An animal form need not represent a specific animal; it may combine features of several animals.

Study the examples in this book to determine the artist's subject, his possible inspiration, his emotional reasons for creating the sculpture, and how successful it is as a result of the material he has chosen to use.

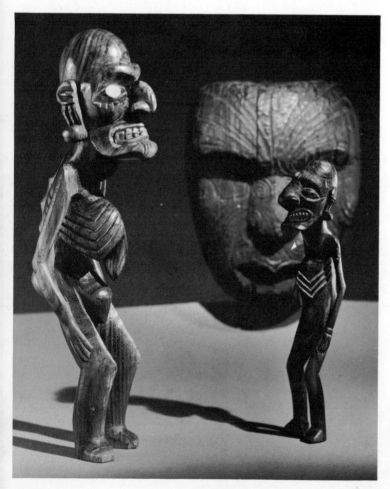

Easter Island Male Figures. Wood. Figures may represent an ancestor on his return after death. Large head at rear is Maori and believed to be a ceremonial object. COURTESY, FIELD MUSEUM OF NATURAL HISTORY, CHICAGO

Weeping Female Figure, Eldon Danhausen. Sentiment is conveyed through a carved walnut wood sculpture. COLLECTION, BRADLEY STEINBERG, CHICAGO

The Blonde Negress, Constantin Brancusi. Wood, travertine and marble combined for texture and beautiful shapes. COURTESY, ART INSTITUTE OF CHICAGO

Plaster carved around and through as an abstract design problem. Student, University of Illinois, Champaign-Urbana.

Walrus, Tguplait of Repulse Bay. Soapstone; shows artist's familiarity with animals in the Eskimo environment. COURTESY, NATIONAL FILM BOARD, CANADA

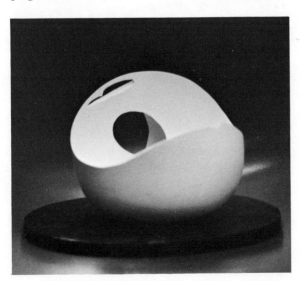

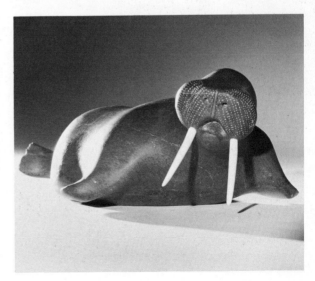

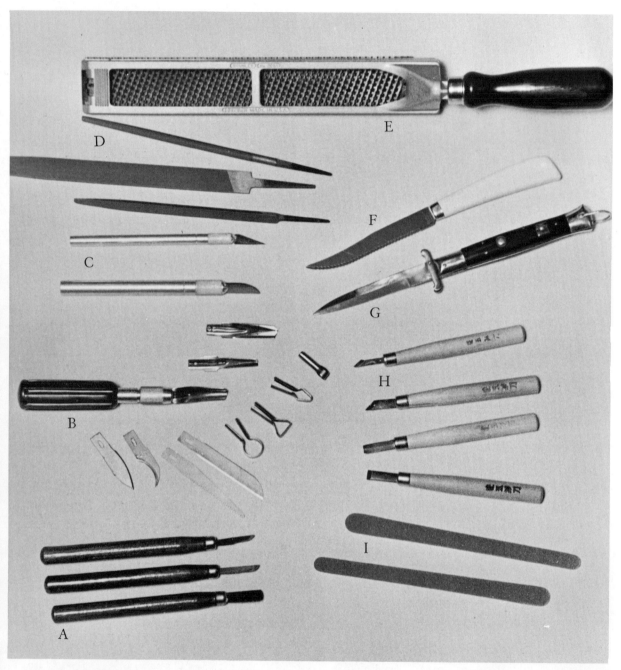

Tools for carving soft materials include: a. small wood carving tools; b. X-acto knife set with interchangeable blades for cutting, routing and gouging all kinds of materials; c. X-acto knives with interchangeable blades for carving, cutting, scribing, etching, etc.; d. files and rasps in various shapes and sizes; e. Surform rasp; f. kitchen paring knife; g. penknife; h. linoleum block cutting tools; i. emery boards.

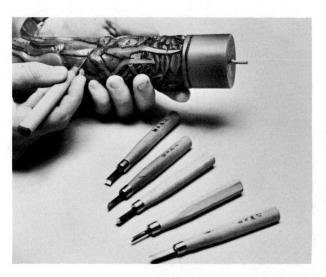

Linoleum-block cutting tools are ideal for carving wax. They can be used for a long time without sharpening because wax is so soft. Carve only up to an inch or so of the candle bottom to allow the candle to fit into the holder. As you work on the candle, it may soften from the heat of your hands, and then it's best to set it aside for a while. Fine lines are sometimes easier to carve when the wax is softer.

To achieve the antiqued, medieval effect shown, acrylic paints are brushed on. Kitchen knives, dental tools and any sharp pointing instruments may be improvised for cutting, as well as the ones shown on page 8.

The paint is gently blended using a cloth or soft paper towel. If too much paint builds up, wipe it off or thin it with water, and blot or spread it. Candles may be sprayed with a thin plastic glaze to keep them clean.

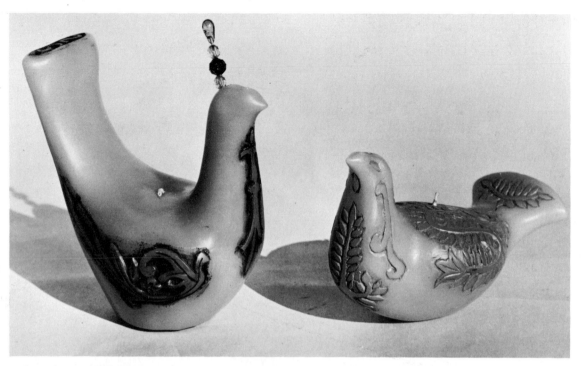

Birds, George Schneider. By carving and painting, the artist has individualized molded candles, which are available in many department stores and candle shops.

Rollouts of "medieval" candles, George Schneider. Although the candle at the left is approximately three inches in diameter and fifteen inches high, it has nine easily recognizable figures on it.

Large blocks may be made by melting several small blocks of paraffin or candles in a pan. When cool remove from pan and carve. This dancing girl was created from melted paraffin by a high school student.

Other carving waxes include blocks of sculptors' modeling and microcrystalline wax. These may be formed into large blocks or sheets for carving. They are made pliable by being run under hot water, or placed beneath a lightbulb, on a warm radiator or in the sun. They may be melted in a pan and poured into a mold, and then the final touches carved. When putting hot wax in a pan or mold, wet the surface of the pan or mold to prevent sticking.

Patterns may be sketched directly, or developed from a drawing or print by placing the print over the wax and cutting through to outline the design on the wax surface.

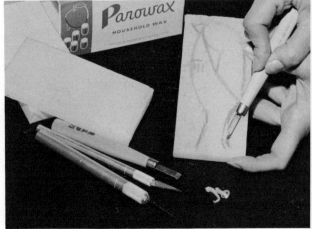

Paraffin blocks are an excellent medium for beginners.

Sculptor John Kearney carves sheets of dental wax and assembles the carved pieces to create a sculpture in wax, using only a paring knife and a heat source to fuse the wax. Such sculptures will last indefinitely providing they are not allowed to get so warm that they melt. Mr. Kearney prefers to have them cast in bronze. Because of the way the carved pieces are assembled, the finished casting has the appearance of an intricate sculpture with a gentle play of negative spaces.

The great advantage of working in wax is that you gain a feeling for mass using a soft material that may be translated into a hard material. Students who will later work with welded metals learn that softened wax reacts in much the same way as softened metal. For casting objects, making the mold directly in wax eliminates a time-consuming step. Usually a sculptor works in clay or plaster. Then a wax mold has to be made before the casting can be poured. Direct wax carving eliminates making the original in the hard material and recreating it in wax.

At first, Kearney warns, it is difficult to think in terms of building up an animal or other form from the inside out in three dimensions. It takes practice, but ultimately develops an invaluable sense of three-dimensional imagery.

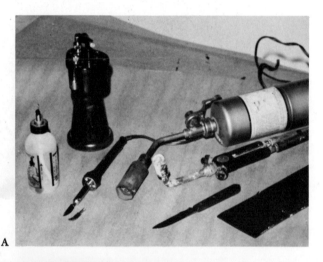

A

Materials include any one or two kinds of heat sources. Shown left to right: a small alcohol torch and a large alcohol torch available from a dental supply house; an electric wax cutting knife, propane torch, oxyacetylene torch, paring knife and sheet of black dental wax.

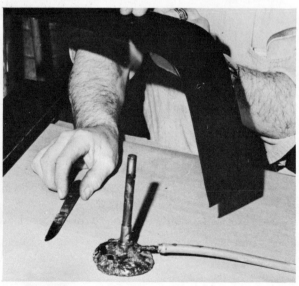

B

Heat the wax until it becomes soft. Heat the knife until it smokes slightly, then carve a series of strips. Both the wax and knife should be heated, or the wax will tend to break.

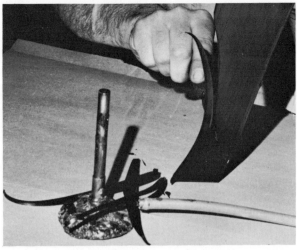

C

Strips are carved according to the shapes needed for the bull's rib cage. Cutting these pieces is much like cutting patterns for a dress.

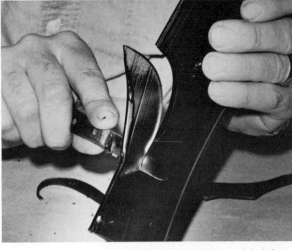

F

Legs are carved. Extra side "I" beams are added for strength and a greater feeling of plasticity.

D

They are fused using the pinpoint flame of the large alcohol torch. (A jeweler's torch may be used also.)

G

As the form emerges, a negative-positive effect of the shapes can be observed.

E

The form is built up with the carved pieces of wax striving for a roundness and feeling of the animal's shape.

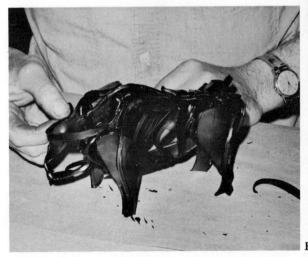

H

Finished animal is glazed by passing a torch gently over the surface to soften edges and make form flow together. Too much heat will collapse the form.

Animals, John Kearney. The finished wax bull from the previous page and a ram and horse that have been cast into bronze by the lost wax technique. This means that the wax melted as the bronze was poured into the molds; hence "lost wax."

Late in life the famous French artist Edgar Degas created small wax sculptures which were found in perfect condition after his death. His heirs had them all cast into bronze; these are two of the finished pieces.

Bust, Edgar Degas. COURTESY, THE METROPOLITAN MUSEUM OF ART, THE H. O. HAVEMEYER COLLECTION

Woman Bathing, Edgar Degas. COURTESY, THE METROPOLITAN MUSEUM OF ART, THE H.O. HAVEMEYER COLLECTION

Soap

Soap carving should not be limited to primary school projects. Soap is so easy to carve and so available that it has tremendous potential for the beginning carver of any age. Even failures don't go to waste; they can always be used for washing. Use paring knives, nail files or linoleum cutters for soap. For color, use colored bars of soap. If a piece breaks, or when parts must be joined, simply wet the knife and hold it against both pieces of soap until they congeal. Some parts may be pegged together with toothpicks. Many artists use soap to perfect a shape—for a nose, a mouth or a foot, for instance—before carving in a more permanent material.

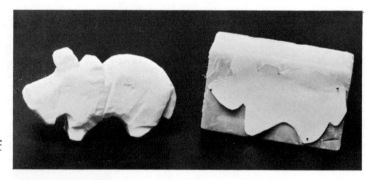

Hippo, David Newfeld, age 8. A bar of Ivory soap is simply blocked out.

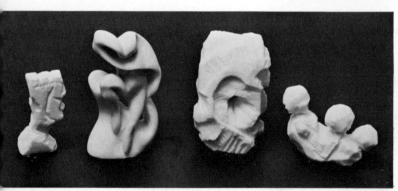

Forms, high school student. Sculpture in the round can be visualized and executed in soap easily.

Squirrel, high school student. Both relief and intaglio methods are incorporated in this squirrel carved from soap. COURTESY, PROCTER AND GAMBLE CO.

Seascape, Milda Morse. Sophisticated carvings can be achieved in soap. Here, several bars of different colors are used. A coat of clear plastic spray glaze protects the surface from dirt.

Adam, Milda Morse.

Mermaid and Diver, Milda Morse

Clay

Clay is one of the oldest sculpture media. An earth product, its consistency varies and requires baking to become hard and permanent. In addition to the many clays available for ceramic and modeling there are new "self-hardening" clays that do not require baking in a kiln. These are ideally suited for the carver, because they are moist and soft for working. When a carving cannot be finished all at once, moisture may held by wrapping the work in a plastic bag. Air-drying time depends upon the size and thickness of the sculpture. When the object is hard, additional carving may be done with files, rasps and stone-carving tools.

Some self-hardening clays are already the consistency normally associated with clay; others are a powder that becomes clay-like when mixed with water. Self-hardening clays air-dry to a bone color and may be finished with paints or covered with metallic finishes.

Ceramic clays require firing in a kiln. They also offer a variety of challenges to the carver, and may be worked with such simple tools as orange sticks, dental tools and any of those shown on page 8. Plastecine clays have an oil base and remain permanently pliable and soft. They are excellent for carving negative molds for casting plaster; the oil in the clay prevents the water-base plaster from sticking to it.*

———

* See *Creating with Plaster,* by Dona Z. Meilach, in this series.

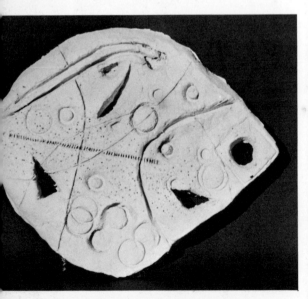

lf-hardening clay carved using lipstick tubes, teeth a comb and other items from a girl's purse. Sherry skin.

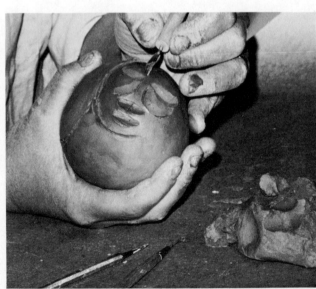

Features are carved with dental tools. Ball was developed with slabs of clay, rather than in one solid ball to facilitate drying and minimize shrinkage.

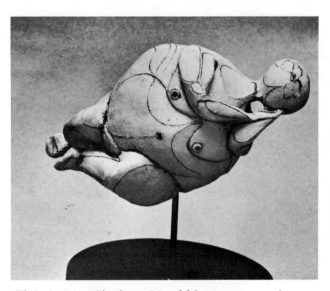

Flaked Out, Charlotte Newfeld. Stoneware clay with dark slip glaze. Baked in a kiln.

Fream Bowl, Robert Pierron. Clay heads rolled in the hand, allowed to become leather-hard, then carved with dental and wax tools, small files and rasps.

Virgin and Child. Terra Cotta. Florentine c. 1490.
COURTESY, ART INSTITUTE OF CHICAGO

Genghis Khan, Erwin Angres

Old Salt, Erwin Angres

At the Market, Erwin Angres

Apple Carving

Carve a golden or red delicious apple, dry it quickly and let it shrink. The result is a sculpture that will last for years and have the texture and appearance of soft wood. When dried properly the apples will not rot.

Apples were carved as a folk art in many early American communities and involved complicated preserving and drying methods. A simple method for apple drying was discovered in the mid-1950's by Chicagoan Erwin Angres when he left a partly peeled apple on a hot radiator. The shrunken apple suggested skin textures, and he began to experiment.

With carved apples you never know what to expect; nature's dehydration is like a happy accident. In addition to heads, apples may be carved into feet and hands with incredible realism. Apple carvings may be mounted on sculpture blocks or on appropriate pieces of driftwood, as shown.

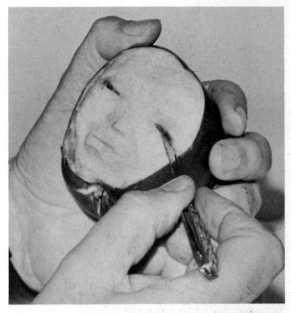

Select a firm apple and pare part of the skin with a paring or penknife, then begin to carve features and facial planes. (You can eat the apple you cut away.) Apples may be treated with lemon juice or other preservative, but it is *not* necessary.

Cut slits for the eyes and embed a piece of the peeling. If you wish to create a hat or hair that stands away from the head, as in the examples at left, partially detach the peeling from the apple and turn under to shape.

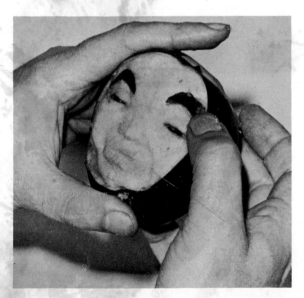

Eyebrows, moustache, tongue, etc., are pieces of scrap apple skin placed in position; no gluing necessary. If the mouth or eyes are to open wide, make the cut deep. The secret of preventing rotting and deterioration is to dehydrate the apple quickly by placing it on a hot-air furnace overnight or in a 120° oven for about one hour. Allow apple to dry

a few more days at room temperature. Sculpture will shrink to about one-third the original size. The resulting "face" (like all faces) is up to nature. When you think the apple is dry, spray with a thin coat of clear plastic glaze. Apples may also be dipped in plastic for a high gloss, but this tends to fill in the wrinkles and hide the inherent texture.

3   Wood Carving

Wood carvings range from tiny whittled figures to huge forms carved from logs. Subjects vary from realistic human and animal forms to completely non-representational statements. Wood has been used as a sculptural medium since ancient times; but because it is an organic material it tends to deteriorate, and few early wood sculptures have survived.

In the twentieth century, however, wood has become more and more popular with sculptors. New finishing and preservative materials promise greater permanence; industrial power saws, drills, sanders, etc., have increased the versatility and potential of the material. The availability of many kinds of exotic woods such as ebony, rosewood, mahogany and others with beautiful grains and easy workability have captured the imaginations of sculptors.

Basically, there are three categories of wood available to the carver—logs, new kiln-dried wood and weathered wood. Logs may be picked up from neighborhoods where trees have been cut down. Some sculptors buy logs from farmers who have had trees cut, or from local nurseries.

The second category of wood, and easiest to obtain, are boards purchased from a lumber yard. These are kiln-dried. Because they are pre-cut, they do limit the size of the carving. However, boards may be laminated (see page 47) to provide a larger carving block.

The third category is wood which has been used, weathered and dried. Such wood can be found where old buildings have been demolished, or from wrecking companies. Old telephone poles and railroad ties can also be bought. Driftwood found along beaches costs nothing; its irregular shapes suggest many forms to the imagination.

For the beginner, a piece of pine is the easiest to work. It cuts sharp and clean, offering little resistance to hand tools. Mahogany and walnut are also favorite woods for carving. The best way to learn about wood and what happens when you begin to carve is through experience. You will find that the direction of the wood's grain will affect the way you cut into it. Cutting with the grain is easier than cutting across the grain, when using hand tools.

The more you work with wood, the more you learn that there are few absolute rules, because wood is an organic entity. The wood of a pine branch, for example, cut in the spring, will differ considerably from the branch of the same tree cut in the fall. There will also be differences in the branches cut from down low or higher up, because of the tree's growth patterns.

About the only absolute statement one can make is that all wood comes from trees. Every sculptor differs in his opinion about the best kind of wood to use, how to work it and what the final statement should be. The techniques and observations presented here represent only a few of the myriad attitudes of sculptors. They should be studied as individual methods of working that will stimulate you to experiment and arrive at your own conclusions about the best way to carve for your own purposes.

People Figures, Student, I.I.T. Lathe-carved pine. PHOTO: RAY PEARSON

Card Players, Don Trachsler. Machine-carved pine, painted. PHOTO: AUTHOR

Untitled, Gerald J Tomany. African mahogany, Korina wood on black base. Hand-carved, laminated. PHOTO: AUTHOR

Dream in Primaries, Mychajlo R. Urban. Locust and applewood, hand-carved and painted. COURTESY, ARTIST

Untitled, Ray Fink. Hand-carved walnut. PHOTO: RAY PEARSON

Woods are classified as softwood or hardwood—but this has little relation to the actual density of the wood and its resistance to carving tools. Softwoods are trees with needle-like leaves, such as pine, fir, hemlock, holly and all evergreens. Hardwoods are broad-leaved trees, such as oak, walnut, mahogany, cherry, ebony, maple and hickory. Most hardwoods tend to splinter less than the softwoods (with the exception of pine, which is great for cutting clean), and are therefore more desirable for most sculptors. However, when power tools are used, splintering isn't as great a problem as when hand carving tools are used.

For a more thorough investigation into the properties of the more than 800 varieties of wood, refer to the U.S. government publications or to books that identify woods by their leaves, flowers or bark patterns. This is particularly important when you are selecting cut logs. It's pointless to haul a huge, heavy log before identifying it. A wood used in furniture-making would be fine for sculpture, but if the wood is the kind used in making crates, it's not worth bringing home.

Tools

Most of the tools shown on page 8 are adaptable to wood carving. In addition, heavier tools specifically made for wood carving are shown below. A catalog from a sculptors' supply source will show the tremendous variety of blade shapes, from narrow and wide straight blades to shallow and deep V and U shapes. New wood carving tools must be sharpened before using; they must be kept razor sharp as you work. Wood carving tools dull quickly; most serious carvers learn to sharpen their own tools, using oil stones and grinding wheels.

Wood carving tools are manipulated by hand or with mallets usually made of lignum vitae, an extremely hard wood. Most carving requires that the wood be clamped to a workbench or held firmly by special positioners. Large logs may be set among sand bags or tied to a tree or post to hold them steady while carving. (Only whittlers work with the wood in their hand, using a very soft wood and sharp penknife.)

Any tools that will do the job are obviously the best to use. These may include assorted tools used by the carpenter, from hand saws, files and rasps, to table saws, jigsaws, etc.

Regardless of the tools used, always follow safety rules strictly. Always work hand tools keeping your hands *behind* the tool and the direction of the cut. *Never* place fingers near the cutting edge of moving saw blades. Never wear long ties, scarves, belts, or hair that may catch in the blade and become entangled.

Wood carving tools; gouges and chisels with various shaped edges, rasps and rifflers, lignum vitae mallet, oil and oil stone for sharpening, sandpaper, emery cloth and steel wool.

Checks, Knots, Grain

Whether you work with logs or kiln-dried lumber, you will encounter certain characteristics of wood that will affect your carving. These are due to the various growth patterns of wood and to the way the wood is dried.

One of the most persistent problems to sculptors is the "checking" or cracks that appear in wood, and particularly in logs that have been air-dried over a period of months or years. Checks occur vertically in a log and vary from slight to deep openings. Wood tends to expand and contract with the humidity of its environment even after it is cut from the tree and is years old. Today, many sculptors will work a log and ignore the checks because they are inherent in the material. A check in no way limits the durability of the wood. Sculptors who object to checks may fill them in with splinters of the same wood or with wood putty.

Knots and burls are the result of branch formations; they may also be ignored or used advantageously. Once a log is stripped of its bark and carving begins, the artist has no way of knowing when a knot will show up within the tree's growth rings. In cut lumber, knots may be avoided by buying select rather than common grades. Burls often have beautiful grain formations around them and may be cleverly worked into the sculptural composition.

Grain is the actual fibrous structure of the wood and is the character which gives wood its distinctive patterns. You can observe grain most readily in a piece of cut lumber; that which runs the length of the board is the "face grain." At the cut ends of the board you will note that the grain is circular; this is the result of cutting across the growth rings of the tree. This is called "end grain." Experiment with tools to learn how different directions of the grain react to cutting.

Cowboy, J. Randall. Sugar pine, whittled. Head and body, arms and saddle are separate pieces of wood glued together.

Two Personages, Barbara Hepworth. Teak with painted and natural finished surfaces. COURTESY, MARL-
BOROUGH FINE ART, LTD. LONDON

Bird, Senufo Tribe, West Africa. 19th century.
COURTESY, CHASE MANHATTAN BANK, NEW YORK

Painted Ceremonial Figure, Maprik Area, New Guinea. 20th century. COURTESY, SEARS VINCENT PRICE GALLERY, CHICAGO

Finishing

Because wood is porous, its surface is usually treated in some way. Depending upon the result desired and the type of wood used, finishing may be done by three basic methods: preserving the natural tone, staining, and coloring.

When a wood has inherent color and beautiful grain—walnut and mahogany, for example—the artist may prefer to give it a transparent finish mainly to keep dust from penetrating the pores. Danish oils,

furniture wax or shellac may be applied to help bring out the grains. With very fibrous woods such as red oak, a coat of epoxy resin may be applied to hold the fibers together and then a polyurethane to seal the wood. If the effect is too glossy, it may be cut down by rubbing on a carnauba wax.

Staining is usually done when the artist wants the original wood color altered. He may have used a light pine because it was less expensive and more easily available than walnut. By applying a walnut stain he can simulate the appearance of the finer

Figure with Drinking Cup, Lower Congo River area, Africa. COURTESY, FIELD MUSEUM OF NATURAL HISTORY, CHICAGO

Cigar Store Indian, American folk art. 19th century. COURTESY, ART INSTITUTE OF CHICAGO

wood. Stain penetrates the pores of the wood; shellac or epoxy transparent finish may then be applied as a preservative.

Color may be as important a means of expression in sculpture as it is in painting; therefore when the entire work or even parts of it are to be painted, it must be treated as when painting any other wooden surface. The raw wood must be sealed with a special paint sealer or shellac and then the paint applied.

Often, after a sculpture is finished, the sculptor changes his mind about the result.

There are many paint-removing products available, as well as wood bleaches. So if you have finished a sculptured surface, you are not permanently committed to that finish. This versatility is one of the advantages of working with wood.

After a sculpture is painted, it should be smoothed. Sandpaper is one method. Experiment with several degrees of roughness and types of grit. To hand-sand, wrap the paper around a block of wood, working first with a rough, then with a finer sandpaper.

Get the feeling of your tools and woods by working on a flat piece of pine clamped with a C clamp to a worktable. Draw a design on the wood and visualize which parts you want carved in relief and which will be cut more deeply than others. Remember your drawing is cut away as you carve.

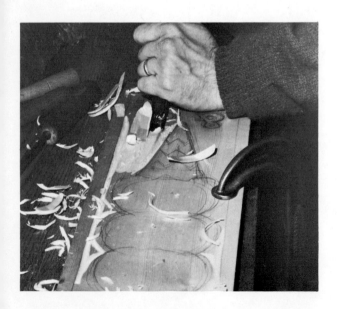

Hold your tool close to the top of the blade with one hand. Direct and push the tool with the other hand. Take up thin slivers. Should the tool embed too deeply just pull the tool back out. Don't pry up the wood or you'll chip the edge of the blade. Try flat chisels, V and U shaped gouges.

Honest Gambling, Edward Larson. Pine. Three surfaces are achieved. The letters project from the background, the border line is gouged more deeply.

Love Conquers, Edward Larson. Pine.

Boxed In, Edward Larson. Pine.

Carved Box, Guatemala. COLLECTION, DON BLAIR, TAOS, NEW MEXICO

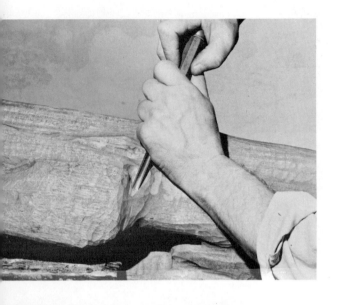

The gouge may be wielded by hand in soft wood; it is particularly useful for working out small areas.

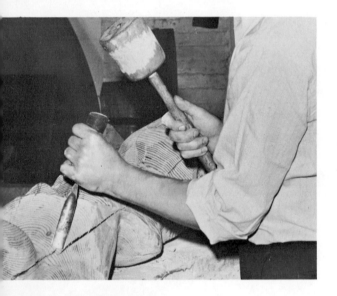

In harder wood, the gouge is worked with a mallet. Note the difference in grain and texture between this oak log and the mahogany log above.

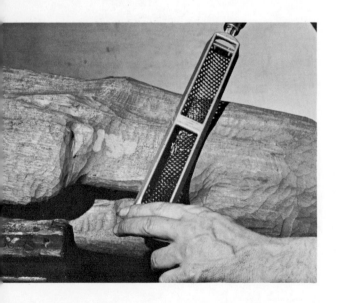

The Surform rasp will smooth and remove wood quickly. Finer rasps and files, and curved tools, are used for corners and small indentations.

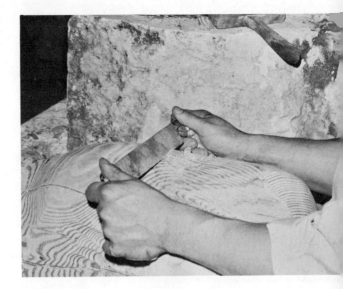

A drawknife will shave large planes.

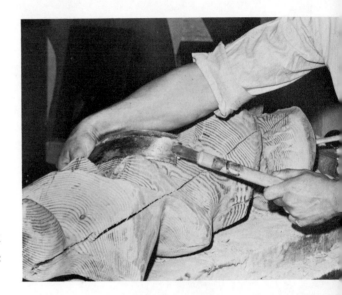

A flexible shaft saw enables you to work around protrusions. Note the checks in the wood.

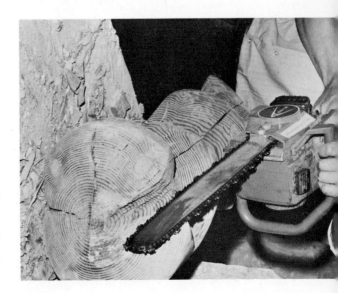

The chain saw will block out large areas quickly. Here you can observe the circular pattern of the end grain, the knots and the different grain patterns along the length of the log.

Easter Island Gods, Marlin Simon. Palm.

After the bark and outer layer are peeled off, the figures are blocked out with an axe, chisels and gouges. Artist Marlin Simon steadies the block by sitting on it. These palm logs have been hauled from the city dump.

May, 1962, Alvin Light. One ingenious way to achieve open spaces in a sculpture created from cylindrical logs is to assemble the parts. Wooden pegs are used. COURTESY, ART INSTITUTE OF CHICAGO

Portrait of the Artist with a Beard, Sidney Simon. Black walnut. Surface texture relies completely on the marks left by the tools. COURTESY, ARTIST

Fertility No. 3, Jullian Frederick Harr. Red oak finished with epoxy resin and polyurethane, then carnauba wax.

Sultan from a Distant Island, Toshio Odate. Oak.
COURTESY, STEPHEN RADICH GALLERY, NEW YORK

Three Slaves, Bernard Simon. African beef wood.
COURTESY, RUTH WHITE GALLERY, NEW YORK

Color Study, Fred Borcherdt. Maple painted with oils, mounted on stone.

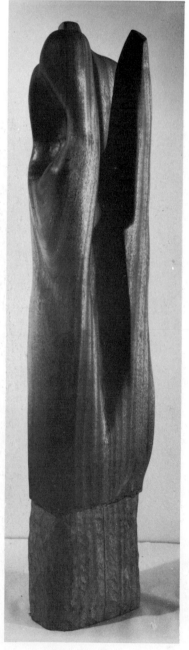

Lineal, Masha Solomon. Mahogany. COURTESY, RUTH
WHITE GALLERY, NEW YORK

Scammon, Oliver Andrews. Pine and bronze.
COURTESY, DAVID STUART GALLERY, LOS ANGELES

Convolution, Mychajlo R. Urban. Locust wood.
PHOTO: W. KOCUROVSKY

Reclining Figure, Henry Moore. Elm wood. COURTESY, ARTIST

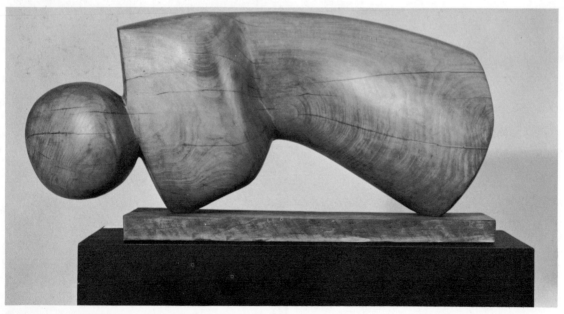

Sculpture, Roald Hague. COURTESY, ART INSTITUTE OF CHICAGO

The Barn, Bernard Langlais. Carved weathered wood relief. PHOTO: RUDOLPH BURCKHARDT

Carving Mechanically

Carving with electrically operated equipment has been a tremendous boon to sculptors who have brought tools used by craftsmen and industry into their studios. Shown below is a lightweight power jigsaw small enough to fit on a typewriter table. With the attachments for a side power motor drive you can have a complete workshop in an amazingly small amount of space. Attachments include a flexible shaft with a hand-held grinding tool, a disc sander, bench grinder and buffing wheel. The versatility of the unit is remarkable. It may be used for shaping plastics, shell, bone, stone and other materials.

Artist Don Trachsler demonstrates the use of the Dremel "Moto-shop" to make the sculptures shown on page 44.

A sketched figure is blocked out of a piece of pine board.

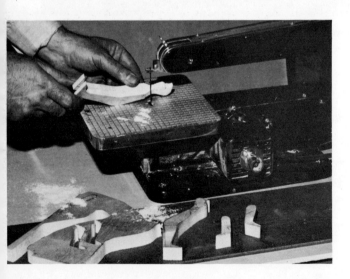

Shaping, as well as straight sawing, is done with the jigsaw blade.

Flat pieces are smoothed on the sanding wheel.

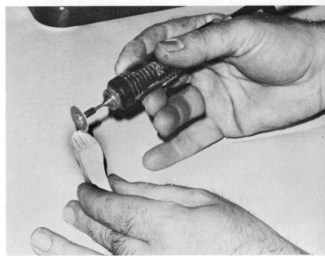

The attached hand piece on a flexible shaft has an assortment of bits and grinding wheels to accomplish any conceivable finishing or detail. Here a cutting disc creates fingers.

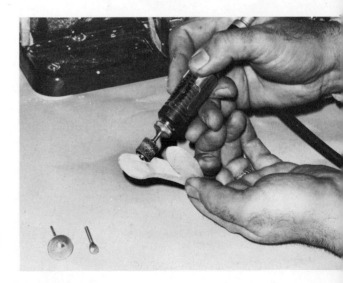

Finer details are accomplished with the appropriate head on the hand grinding tool. Parts are glued together and painted.

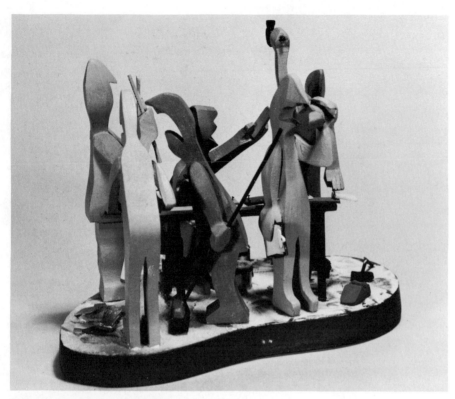

The Builders, Don Trachsler

The Scribe, Don Trachsler

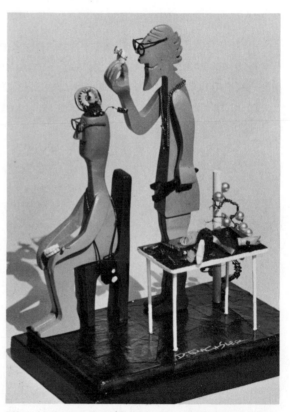

The Analyst and the Dentist, Don Trachsler. COLLEC-
TION, DR. AND MRS. MELVIN M. MEILACH, CHICAGO

Totem, Bernard Langlais. COLLECTION, MR. THOMAS FOLD, NEW YORK. COURTESY, LEO CASTELLI GALLERY, NEW YORK

Mount Rainier, Robert E. Hopkins, Jr.
COURTESY, SEATTLE ART MUSEUM

Saw Sculptures

Carpenter's tools such as the table saw, jigsaw, band saw and others may be used for many wood sculptures. Shown below are a few of the infinite forms that can be made with a table saw.

Begin with a rectangular block of wood or a dowel. Make regular cuts on one surface, then change the angle of the blade and make another cut to meet the first. Turn the block on another side and make another series of cuts. With a little experimentation, you'll be amazed at the beautiful forms that result.

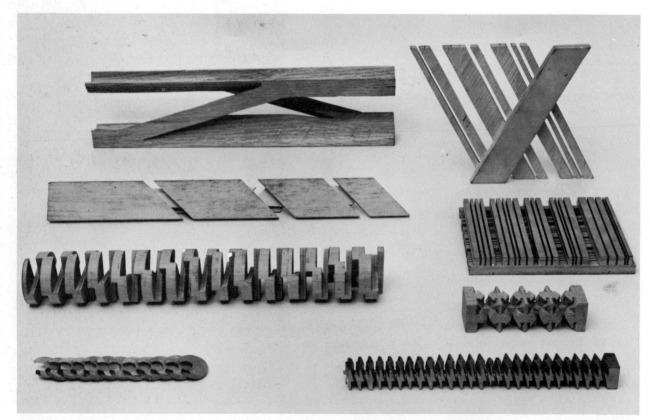

Table saw sculptures. Students, Institute of Design, I.I.T., Chicago. PHOTO: RAY PEARSON

Laminating

Laminating consists of gluing together cuts of wood. By using woods with different colors and patterns and by running the grains in opposite or right-angle directions, the finished sculpture will have a varied surface appearance that is impossible to achieve any other way. Boards to be laminated must be carefully sawed and perfectly flat (not warped) to make a perfect bond. Use white emulsion, epoxy or resorcin glues for laminating. Glued boards must be clamped and allowed to dry thoroughly before sawing or hand carving.

Student, University of Illinois, Champaign-Urbana. The varying directions of grain and oddly shaped forms are possible by laminating.

Family, Doris Chase. Laminated oak. Laminated wood may be worked exactly as a solid piece of wood. COURTESY, RUTH WHITE GALLERY, NEW YORK

A hand-held power belt sander is used to smooth a block of laminated boards. You can see the lamination in the end grain of the woods.

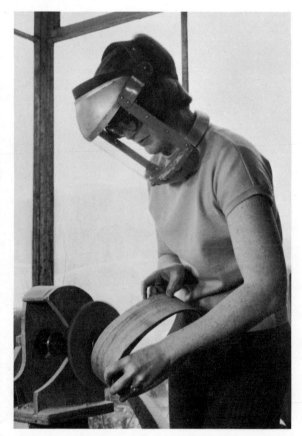

Doris Chase's workshop has "whatever tools she can find to help her create her sculptures." Here she uses a power saw and at right a sanding wheel. She wears a safety mask for protection against wood chips and sawdust. PHOTO SERIES: COURTESY, ARTIST

Interchangeable Forms, Doris Chase. Laminated fir. COURTESY, RUTH WHITE GALLERY, NEW YORK

Bird Keys, Gabriel Kohn. Laminated wood with pegs. COURTESY,
MARLBOROUGH-GERSON GALLERY, NEW YORK

Six Women, Marisol. Lamination, carving and construction. COURTESY, SIDNEY JANIS GALLERY, NEW YORK

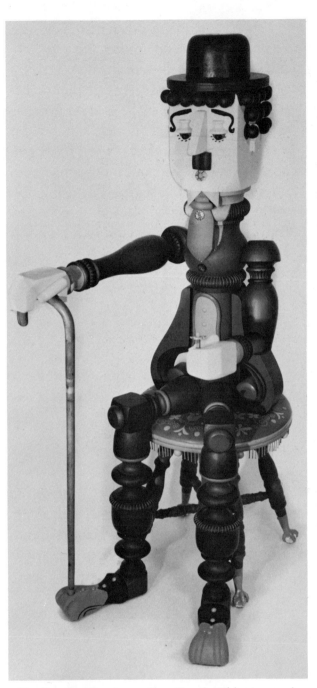

Charlie Chaplin, Jacqueline Fogel. Old pieces of
bannisters, posts and found wood have been carved,
reassembled and painted. PHOTO: RUPERT FINEGOLD

Costruzione, Tomonori Toyofuku. COURTESY,
GALLERIA D'ARTE DEL NAVIGLIO, MILAN

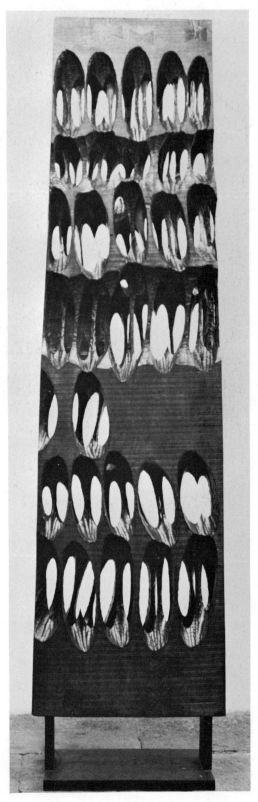

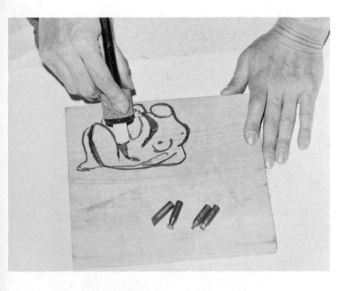

Wood, and many other materials such as plastic, horn and leather, may be subtracted, or carved, by burning unusual compositions and textures. Any of the torches shown on page 14 may be used for burning wood; decide which is the best tool for your purpose. One of the easiest for beginners to use is the woodburning pencil with assorted widths and shapes of burning tips. All techniques shown may also be successfully used in carving a wood block for printmaking.

When burning with an oxyacetylene torch, brush the ash of the wood with a wire brush. Plywood, which is laminated in thin layers, can be burned through to the various layers for a variety of grains.

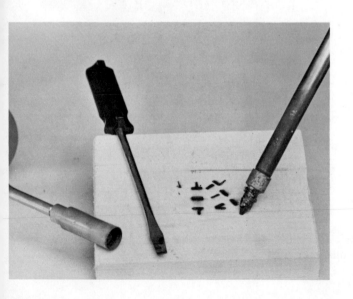

Heated instruments used for carving are a soldering iron, a calrod, or a screwdriver that has been heated by a torch and impressed in the materials.

Large Burnt Wood, Alberto Burri. COLLECTION, MRS. ARNOLD MAREMONT, WINNETKA, ILLINOIS

Abstract,
Margaret Gessel

Untitled, Robert Pierron. Layered plywood shredded and completely burned through.

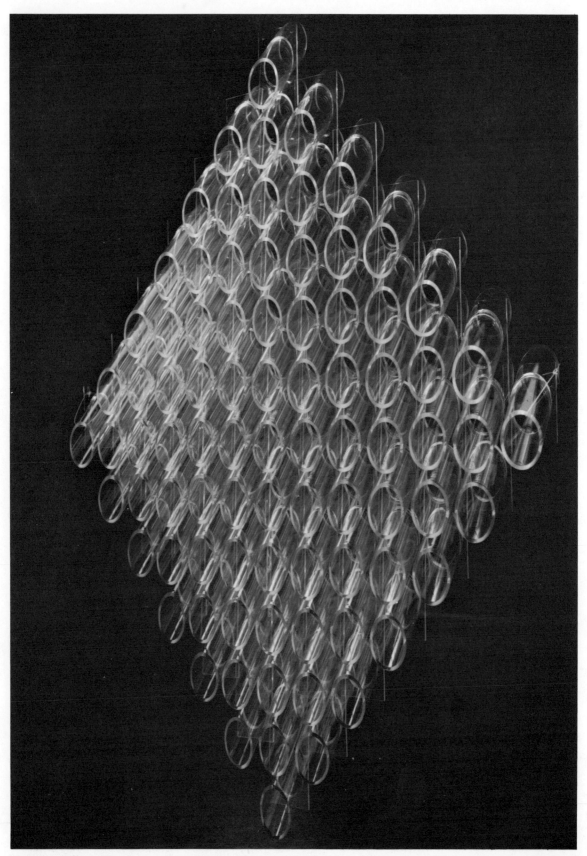

Untitled, Lillian Florsheim. Clear Plexiglas sheets and tubes. COLLECTION, MR. AND MRS. SAMUEL J. POPEIL, CHICAGO. PHOTO: LIPNER.

Acrylic plastic, a man-made material used mainly by industry, came into our vocabulary in the 1930's. We know it best as a clear, hard plastic in sheets or rods. A few artists such as Moholy-Nagy and Naum Gabo experimented with the properties of acrylic plastic in the 1930's and began to employ them in the arts.

In the last few years sculptors have further investigated the potentials of the plastics, experimented and adapted them to meaningful artistic expressions. The use of plastics in the arts is increasing. A few plastic manufacturers are donating scrap plastics to art schools, and the results show a variety of promising directions for artistic activity.

Many artists say they would like to try plastics as a medium, but fear it is complicated and requires a good knowledge of

Untitled, Student, Clear acrylic block, machine-carved.

chemistry. This is not so. One sculptor interviewed checked his yellow pages, ordered $30.00 of scrap plastic from a local company and was soon happily immersed in cutting, drilling, laminating and shaping.

Acrylic plastics (Plexiglas is one brand) are made in an assortment of colors and textures that may be combined for unusual results. Plastics can be worked with the same electric cutting tools you use for wood; the only caution is that the cut parts must be held apart, because the heat of the blades' friction may cause the edges to melt and reseal.

Acrylic plastic is available in sheets, solid rods and tubes. Sheets are covered with adhesive paper to prevent scratching; this paper forms an ideal surface for marking your cuts.

Plastic may be drilled using hand or power drills. Edges may be smoothed with sandpaper.

Plastics may be joined and even laminated as wood. They require a specific plastic solvent rather than glue. Plastic adhesion depends upon the intermingling of the molecules of the joined surfaces. To effect this intermingling and cohesion, the surfaces to be joined are softened with the solvent. After adhesion occurs, the solvent evaporates, the material hardens again and a clear joint results.

Plastics may be worked in many different ways: thermo formed, combined with other materials, used as painting surfaces and for printing blocks. In these pages we are concerned with plastic as a carving medium.

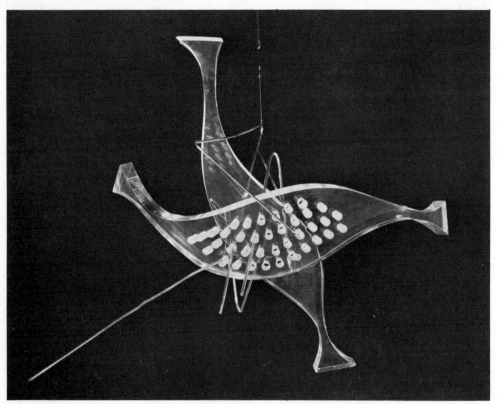

Fish, László Moholy-Nagy. Suspended form, clear acrylic plastic. COURTESY, ART INSTITUTE OF CHICAGO

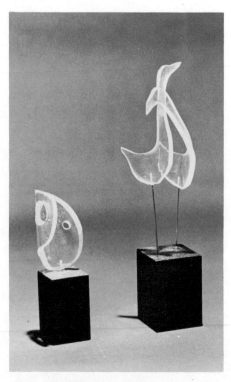

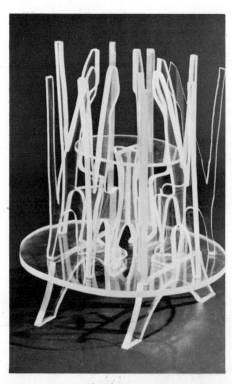

Birds, Don Trachsler. Clear Plexiglas.   *The Card Players,* Don Trachsler

Bull, John Kearney. Black dental wax.
PHOTO: AUTHOR

Formica #15, Dennis Jones. Laminated plastic and machine-carved wood. PHOTO: THOMAS ZAMIAR

Carved apples, Erwin Angres. PHOTO: AUTHOR

Cuadrado, Dona Meilach. Machine-carved colored acrylic. PHOTO: AUTHOR

Carved wax candles, four candles by George Schneider, candle second from right by Robert W. Anderson. PHOTO: AUTHOR

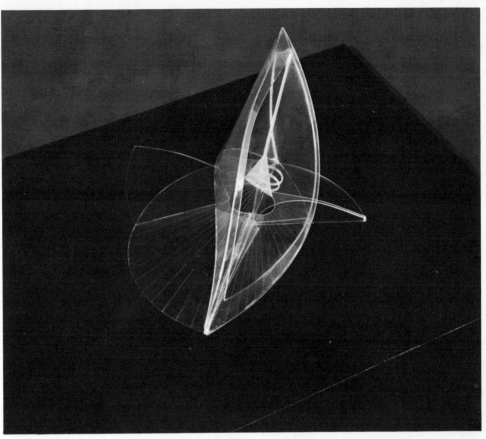

Spiral Theme, Naum Gabo. COURTESY, MUSEUM OF MODERN ART, NEW YORK

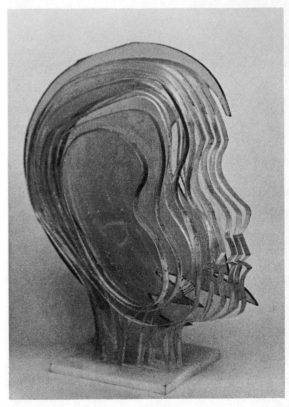

Young Girl, John Kearney. Various sizes and shapes
of carved blue plastic, laminated.

Acrylic plastic sheets have a paper backing on which designs can be drawn, as shown. (To trace a design, remove the paper, place the plastic over the design and draw directly on the plastic.) Plastic samples can be ordered from companies listed in a telephone book. A special liquid solvent for bonding plastic is shown.

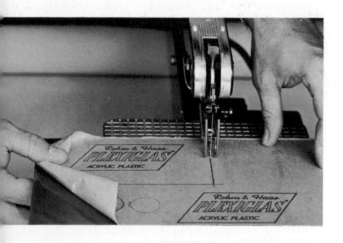

Plastic sheets and tubes can be cut on the jigsaw, table saw, etc. The resulting dust should be vacuumed.

Holes can be made with a hand drill or with machine drilling tools.

Plastic has a low melting point and can be shaped successfully using the heat from an oven. Place a baking dish in a 300° oven. Set the plastic in the heated dish and close the oven for about eight minutes. Wear heat-resistant gloves, and test the plastic to see if it's pliable. If not, heat it a couple of minutes longer.

When the plastic is ready, remove it from the oven and shape it quickly while it's hot because the material cools and hardens in minutes. (It can be bent around another shape for curves and sharp angles.) If a satisfactory bend is made before the material hardens sufficiently, run it under cold water to set.

Bond sanded edges by brushing the solvent or applying with a stick (it sets within seconds). For intricate spots, use a glass eyedropper to apply the solvent.

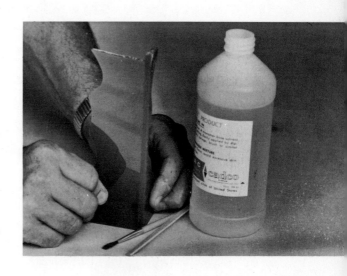

Untitled, Lillian Florsheim. Clear and opaque white plastic.
PHOTO: W. B. NICKERSON

Compositions with carved opaque white plastic by students of the Institute of Design, I.I.T., Chicago

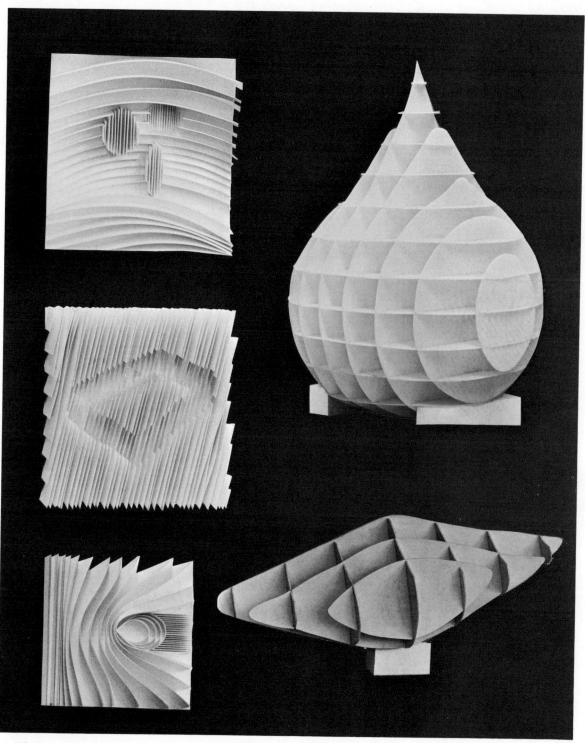

Plastic constructions created by sawing to shape and heating to bend, by students of the Institute of Design, I.I.T., Chicago

The Tourists. Carved plastic foam, by students of the University of Illinois, Champaign-Urbana

Plastic Foam

Among the many types of plastics being investigated for artistic use are the family of polystyrenes, usually referred to as Styrofoam, although available under many brand names. Plastic foams are made of the same materials as the solid acrylic plastics —coal, petroleum, natural gas and other materials—but during the manufacturing process the cells are blown up with gas. The result varies with the type of process used, so that foams may be rigid or flexible, hard or soft, open-celled or closed-celled. They are all extremely lightweight and very strong; most are fireproof.

The rigid foams are used by the sculptor because they may be cut, carved, assembled, glued and painted. Plastic foam usually should be covered with a coating of gesso, plaster, modeling paste or putty before painting, because some paints eat up the foam. The carved, coated foam, when smoothed and painted, resembles stone or metal sculpture. It may be given a hard coating such as fiber glass saturated with polyester resin, shellac or a plastic glaze.

Because foams melt under heat, but do not burn, they are often used in the same way as wax for creating castings. The method has come to be known as "lost foam" casting.

Foams are available as blocks and sheets in many sizes, and have widely differing densities, which should be noted by the sculptor. There are very porous foams, such as those used by florists, and there are some so solid they have the appearance of a piece of stone.

Plastic foam may be cut with any sharp instrument—saws, knives, etc.—but they are easiest to cut with a heated blade. Craft shops have special hot wire cutters that resemble a jigsaw, except the blade is heated and stationary. These can handle large blocks of foam. The hot blade also can be inserted into the center of a block, should an interior hole be needed. X-acto has a small heated blade tool for carving foam. You can also use a soldering iron or a blade that has been held in a flame for a few seconds.

When gluing and painting, use products that are compatible with the plastic foam; some glues as well as paints will tend to disintegrate the cellular structure of the foam. Always test your materials on scraps first.

Any tool that will do the job is the proper tool for working any material. An electric soldering iron may be used for making small holes, or for smoothing cut edges.

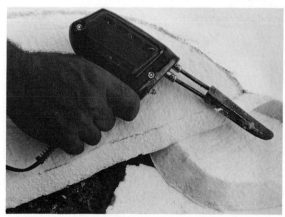

For cutting large sheets of foam, sculptor Albert Vrana has improvised his own heated unit by soldering a sharp blade to the rods of an electric soldering gun.

Like wood, plastic foam may be laminated. The object, though, is to obtain larger blocks; there are no grains or designs to be achieved. Use white emulsion glues (Elmer's, Wil-Hold, etc.). Clamp the glued blocks together to set, using buffer pieces of wood under the clamps to avoid denting the foam.

Any tools used for wood may be used with plastic foams. This laminated foam block has such a high density that it appears almost solid; it is easier to work with rasps than the more porous foams. Foam shavings tend to cling to everything, making clean-up an annoyance.

Drawing for the sculpture begun above. Students, Insitute of Design, I.I.T., Chicago

Auto-body putty has been applied to the shaped piece to give it solidity. It will be smoothed by sanding and painted with a high-gloss white enamel.

Block, Student, Institute of Design, I.I.T., Chicago. Laminated, carved and painted plastic foam.

Untitled, Stephen Weed. Laminated foam, left rough, simulates porous stone.

Falling Dot on Floating Form, Ted Egri. A more porous foam is used here than in the examples above.

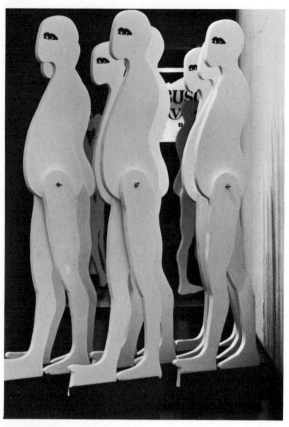

Larger than Life. Styrofoam. PHOTOGRAPHED AT THE KRANNERT ART MUSEUM, UNIVERSITY OF ILLINOIS, CHAMPAIGN-URBANA

With All the Trimmings, Student, University of Illinois, Champaign-Urbana. Plastic foam colored with tempera paints.

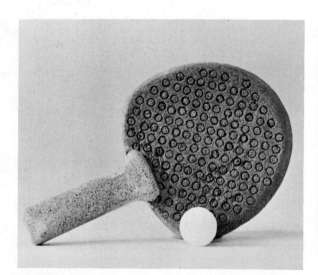

Paddle and Ball, Student, Institute of Design, I.I.T., Chicago. Styrofoam.

Chicken En Route, Ted Egri. Styrofoam body with shaped cardboard for neck and head.

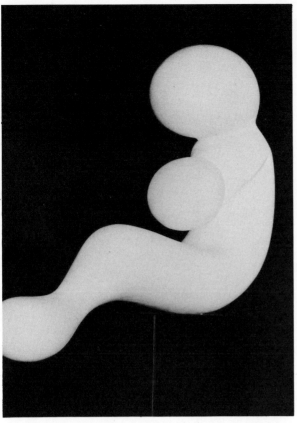

Mother and Child, Student, Institute of Design, I.I.T., Chicago. High-density foam carved in simple amoeboid shapes.

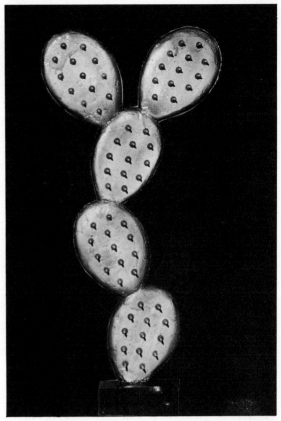

Cactus, Student, Institute of Design, I.I.T., Chicago. Foam leaves with colored thumbtacks to represent needles.

Simon Says, Student, Institute of Design, I.I.T., Chicago. Styrofoam with plaster and paint.

Block Carving, Harriet Arenson. Foam Glas, a plastic foam product, is lightweight, easy to carve.

Miami, Florida, sculptor Albert Vrana has effectively adapted materials of industry for sculptural use. Here, plastic foam (Dyplast) is being carved, hand sanded, ground and assembled for a mold to be cast in concrete for the facade of the building on the opposite page.

The carved pieces are pegged together according to a blueprint. PHOTOS: COURTESY, ALBERT VRANA

Professional Arts Center, Miami, Florida. Cast in concrete from plastic foam (Dyplast). 1966. Albert Vrana, sculptor. PHOTO: BLACK-BAKER

The Kiss, Constantin Brancusi. Stone, 1908. COURTESY, PHILADELPHIA MUSEUM OF ART

5 Stone Carving

Though carving in stone dates back to pre-history, twentieth-century artists are rediscovering stone as a medium for artistic expression. During the nineteenth century, stone statues and architectural decor were the work of stonemasons who reproduced an artist's model from clay, plaster or drawings. The artist himself did not work directly with the material, and the general concensus is that sculptural expression suffered as a result.

Early in the twentieth century when Jean Arp, Constantin Brancusi, Max Bill, Barbara Hepworth, Henry Moore and other sculptors began working directly with stone, the impact on art was tremendous. Stimulated by the simple forms of primitive sculptures, artists rejected the tradition of the academicians and their often trite, unoriginal, realistic sculptural forms.

In searching for new shapes and methods, the artist literally had to begin at the beginning. He had no precedents to follow, no teacher to show him how to work with his materials for his specific purposes. His experiments and innovations blossomed into sculptures representative of the increasingly diverse artistic trends: cubism, abstract expressionism, futurism and others.

The sculptor who works in stone today continually innovates and searches for new ways to exploit this ancient material. Certainly stone is not as easy a carving medium as soap or wax; but, though it offers more resistance to the tool, it need not be foreboding. Stone varies from soft soapstones and featherocks to hard granites, from pebbles to huge boulders.

The beginning carver should select a soft unfigured marble or limestone that is not too flaky. Avoid granite or other extremely hard stones which are difficult to carve. Intricately figured marbles should be avoided too, because the beauty of figuring is so great, the form may become secondary. The shape of a stone often will suggest an abstract form. Minimal carving to further define the form and some polishing may be all that is required.

You might also approach stone carving by working on small rocks you can find near water. Pick up several kinds and sizes, scratch them with a nail and rub with sandpaper. You'll observe that some are much softer than others; any that scratch and sand easily are generally carvable. Some will work as easily as a piece of wood.

A basic knowledge about the formation of stone will help you understand why some are easier to carve than others. Stone falls into three classifications: igneous, sedimentary and metamorphic.

Igneous: formed by the action of fire; extremely hard. Granites and basalts.

Sedimentary: formed by the action of water, by or from deposits of sediment, and found on the beds of lakes and seas. The directions of the stratifications must be considered when carving. Limestones and sandstones.

Metamorphic: igneous and sedimentary stones that have been changed physically by natural forces of pressure, heat and chemistry. Marble, soapstone, slate, alabaster, onyx and all gem stones.

The Scribe Amenhotep, Egyptian. COURTESY,
FIELD MUSEUM OF NATURAL HISTORY, CHICAGO

Seated Buddha, Nagapattinam. Stone, South India
11th century A.D. COURTESY, ART INSTITUTE OF CHICAGO

Testing the Stone

Pieces of stone can be tested for flaws that may make them unsatisfactory for carving. To the carver, flaws would be cracks, soft streaks, veins and stratification that might cause the stone to deteriorate quickly. The first test is to tap the stone with a steel hammer. If the sound rings clear, the piece should be all right. If the sound is a dull thud, the stone is considered "dead" and is unsuitable for carving.

Another test is to wet the entire stone with water. A deep-grained dark streak which seems to go all the way around or through the piece is usually an indication of a crack or layer that may cause the stone to break in the same way as a layer cake.

Watch for other flaws such as pebbles, pockets and fossils that have become embedded in the stone during its metamorphic process.

Where to Get Stone

Stones of different sizes, varieties and shapes are relatively easy to obtain if you know where to look. Check the yellow pages for companies that sell stone. Prices depend upon the kind and size of rock. Many quarries sell stone to artists, and may even cut them to size. Slate, featherock and flagstone are available where gardening supplies are sold. Sculpture suppliers stock marbles, soapstone, wonderstone and others, but unless you live close to them, shipping can be costly. Excellent qualities of marble, limestone and many other stones can be found in wrecked buildings or in yards of wrecking companies who are often happy to sell a stone very cheaply if you cart it away. Tombstone companies also have scraps of good quality marbles. Beautiful gem stones may be found in areas frequented by "rock hounds."

David, Michelangelo. Marble, 1501-1504.
COURTESY, ALINARI-ART REFERENCE BUREAU

Ancient Figure, Brancusi. Limestone,
1906. COURTESY, ART INSTITUTE OF CHICAGO

Carving

The organization of a form in three dimensions gives a piece its sculptural vitality. Once you are able to visualize a form nestling, embryo-like, within the rock, you are ready to carve. You may approach the stone by sketching directly on it and continuing to re-sketch as you carve away. You may wish to organize the form by making a wax or soap model first. Hand tools (shown on pages 76 and 77) include a variety of chisels with flat blades and points, bush hammers, picks and iron mallets. Stone carving with hand tools is a slow process, with only small pieces of the stone removed at a time, as compared to the large pieces you can remove by sawing and chiseling wood. Stone sculptures, especially large pieces, may take weeks, even months, and require patience and painstaking work.

Some power tools can be used on stone. There are pneumatic roto-hammers with points shaped as on hand tools. Circular saws, drills, sanders and grinders may also be used in certain phases of carving, finishing and polishing. A drill with masonry bits may be used for removing large chunks, or to open up a concave area.

Should you encounter a vein while carving, you'll find that it may be harder than the stone itself. In a piece of white marble, for instance, the vein may be yellow or red and have a different composition. The area around the vein is usually soft and crumbly, so it must be worked carefully. Avoid carving the vein itself if possible, even allowing it to protrude slightly from the stone.

Tools should be kept sharp by working their edges on a grindstone. Tempered steel blades require retempering occasionally to

Marble Relief, Maya Culture, Mexico. Late Classic period 1300 A.D. COURTESY, ART INSTITUTE OF CHICAGO

strengthen the steel. Tempering consists of heat-treating the tool to achieve maximum combined strength and hardness. If you don't have the facilities for grinding and tempering, tools may be taken to a sculpture supply source for sharpening. Do not oil tools used for stone carving, as oil tends to stain stones.

Wear safety goggles or a face shield when chipping stone. Dust masks are available with gauze refills to filter out the powdery particles that result from filing and sanding. This is especially important for granite carving, as granite particles can cause lung ailments.

The techniques and tools for carving all stone are essentially the same, with the exception of the harder granites. These require a much heavier set of hammers and carbide-tipped tools (see page 76).

Finishing Stone

Some carvers prefer to leave stone rough, just as it is finished by pointing tools, bush hammers and chisels, often playing one texture against another for greater surface interest. Others prefer a smooth, slick surface or a combination of rough and smooth. For soft stone, files and rasps will refine and smooth the rough surfaces. The piece is then rubbed with pumice or other rubbing stones. It is refined further by rubbing with wet-dry sandpaper, carborundum papers and polishing powders. A final coat of automobile wax or furniture wax, or a thin coat of good quality cement or terrazzo sealer, protects the surface. Many of the silicone products on the market may be sprayed or brushed on. Buffing the sculpture will give it a high shine.

Madonna and Child, Henry Moore. Hornton stone, 1943-44. COURTESY, ARTIST

This short historical survey illustrates the hundreds of years and the various styles through which stone carving has passed in different ages and parts of the world.

Seated Figure, Jacques Lipchitz. Limestone, 1917.
COURTESY, ART INSTITUTE OF CHICAGO

Stone carving tools are (from left to right) bush hammer (also made with a pick at one end), iron hammer made in weights from 1 to 2½ pounds, toothed chisels, also called frosting tools, that are made in several widths and numbers of points, pointed chisel, flat and angled chisels, curved rasps and rifflers. All are hand-forged tempered steel. Refer to sculpture supply catalogs for the range of tools available.

Granite-carving tools are much heavier than those for marble (above) and other stones. The points are essentially the same shape as the marble tools, but they have carbide tips for hardness. These tools may be used on marble; but the reverse—using marble tools on granite—will dull them quickly.

In addition to pneumatic hammers and chisels, a revolving saw blade with different discs may be used to cut and smooth a piece of marble.

The point, held at about a 45° to 90° angle to the block, is used to rough out the form from the block. The tool is held firmly, but not too tightly, about midway down the shank. The hammer is swung freely with the other hand.

Work at a height comfortable for walking around the piece and carving from any side. The carving should take advantage of the original size and shape of the block so as not to waste material or require more work than necessary.

This frosting tool has nine points and is used to create texture.

The narrower toothed frosting tool may be lightly tapped along the stone to create a lined effect.

All marble demonstrations by Egon Weiner.

The point may also be directed, lightly, straight at the stone to create texture. Note the veins in the marble.

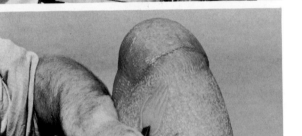

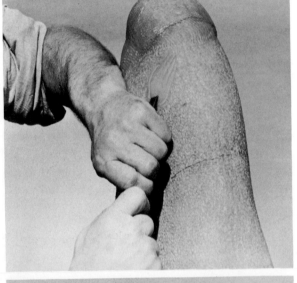

A flat chisel is hand directed for smoothing.

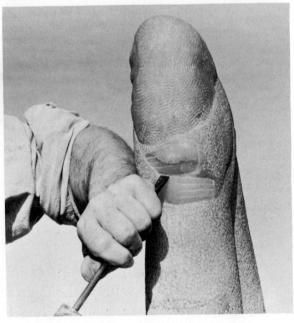

Use the flat chisel with the mallet to create lines.

A long point is hammered for the rough blocking and texturing.

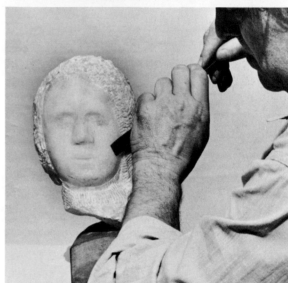

Tool marks are smoothed away with a flat chisel.

A curved rasp helps to shape the chin. The sculpture is mounted by first making a hole in the bottom of the stone, using a star drill, then inserting a rod into the stone and into the wood.

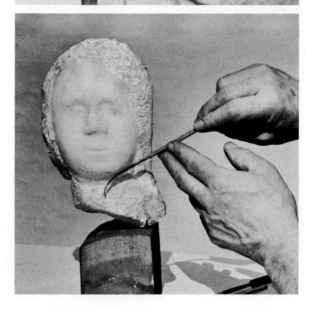

Recumbent Figure, Henry Moore. Green Hornton stone. COLLECTION, THE TATE GALLERY, LONDON. COURTESY, ARTIST

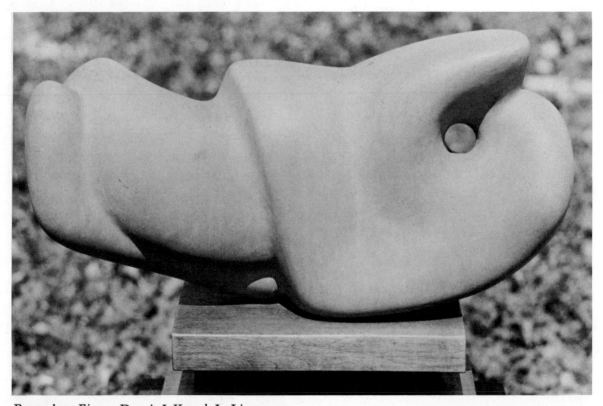

Recumbent Figure, Dennis J. Kowal, Jr. Limestone.

Anthropomorphic Corkscrew,
Dennis J. Kowal, Jr. Limestone.

Image, Barbara Hepworth. Hopton Wood stone.
COURTESY, MARLBOROUGH FINE ART, LTD., LONDON

Construction Out of Circular Ring, Max Bill. Black granite. COURTESY, ART INSTITUTE OF CHICAGO

Extremity of Mythical Wineskin, Jean Arp. Rose granite.
COURTESY, ART INSTITUTE OF CHICAGO

Head of a Prophet, William Zorach. Stone. COURTESY, ART INSTITUTE OF CHICAGO

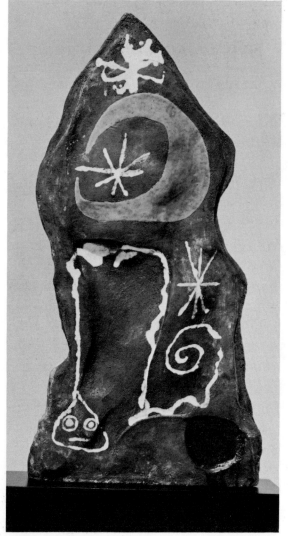

Stone, Joàn Miro. Stone with ceramic coloring. COURTESY, ART INSTITUTE OF CHICAGO

Pastorale, Barbara Hepworth. White marble. COLLECTION, RIJKSMUSEUM KRÖLLER-MÜLLER, HOLLAND. COURTESY, MARLBOROUGH FINE ART LTD., LONDON

Marble

The family of metamorphic stone, consisting of marble, alabaster, onyx, travertine, etc., is most popular for sculpture today. These stones are softer and easier to carve than the granites, and more durable than limestones and other sedimentary rocks. Their variety of colors and textures is endless. You'll find them in varying tones of transparent, translucent and opaque whites, blues, greens, pinks, grays and blacks. You'll also find them with figured, mottled, veined and striped characteristics.

Each stone presents problems typical of and peculiar to its natural formation. Onyx, because it exists in layers, has unpredictable fracturing charactistics. Travertine is very porous because of its sedimentary inheritance and presents the carver with a set of characteristics entirely different from onyx.

Marble from Tennessee is extremely hard and more difficult to carve and polish than marble from other sources. Vermont marble is fine-grained in a variety of colors: reddish, greenish, bluish, creamy and mottled white. Carrara marble from Italy is considered the finest carving marble. Alabama marble resembles Carrara marble but frequently has veinings that make it impractical for carving. A sculptor who has ready access to and likes Georgia marble will find deep-seated blemishes that he may have to work around.

When selecting marble, one must have an idea whether the finished piece will be used indoors or out-of-doors and choose the best material for the weather conditions. Sun may change the color of some varieties. Soot and smoke particles are particularly injurious to marble. Where the temperature falls below freezing, water and moisture will become ice and expand, causing the stone to rot and flake. Generally, the harder and finer grained marbles are selected for out-of-door use in moderate climates. Travertine, which is especially porous, is not recommended for outdoor sculpture. However, many of the silicone products on the market today may be sprayed or brushed on marble and other porous stones to make them comparatively waterproof.

No blanket statement can be made about marbles and how to carve them. So long as the material is made by nature, one must expect the vicissitudes of nature to exist. Coping with these vicissitudes is best learned by experience and is part of the appeal of these materials.

Carving, Henry Moore. Travertine marble. COURTESY, ARTIST

Leda, Constantin Brancusi. Marble on plaster base. COURTESY, ART INSTITUTE OF CHICAGO

Organic Structure, Eldon Danhausen. Marble and brass. COURTESY, ARTIST

Apartheid Irony, Ruth Ingeborg Andris. Italian crystal white alabaster.

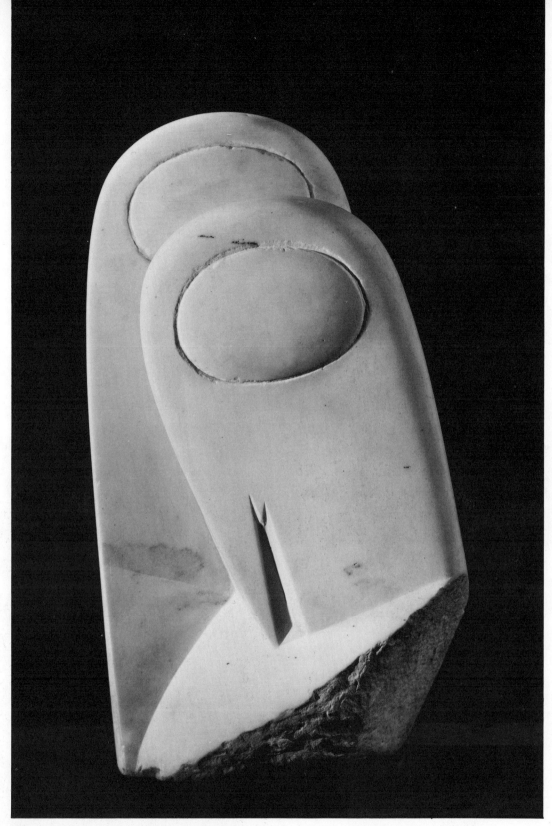

Two Penguins, Constantin Brancusi. White marble. COURTESY, ART INSTITUTE OF CHICAGO

Woman Holding Her Breast, Jullian Frederick Harr. Unpolished marble.

The Stem, Bernard Simon. Pink alabaster. COURTESY, RUTH WHITE GALLERY, NEW YORK

Monte Alban, Oxaca, Mary K. Dowse. Intaglio plaster relief. PHOTO: AUTHOR

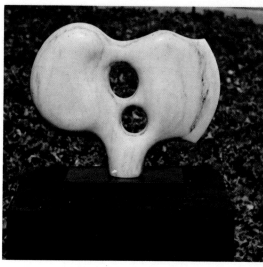

Stone Wave, Dennis J. Kowal, Jr. Marble.
PHOTO: AUTHOR

Birdstone, Indian, 19th century. Steatite.
COLLECTION & PHOTO, RAY PEARSON

Femininity, Don Seiden. Lime-stone. PHOTO: RAY PEARSON

Gemstone Birds, Abby Wadsworth. Adventurtine, Brazil sodalite.
PHOTO: AUTHOR

Torso, Egon Weiner. Marble figure with mirrors to reflect all sides.

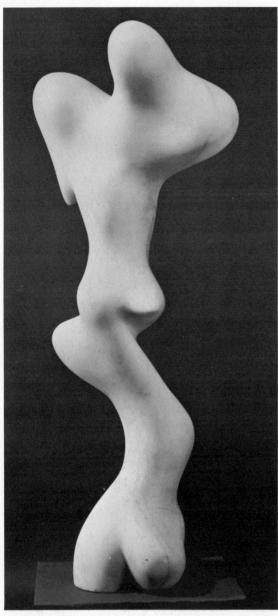

Growth, Hans Arp. White marble. COURTESY, ART INSTITUTE OF CHICAGO

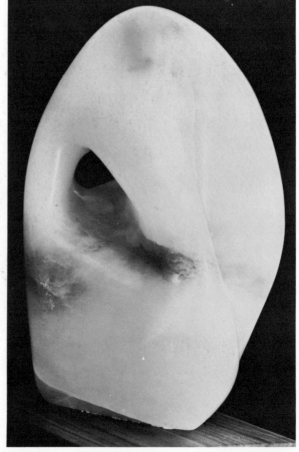

Breakthrough, Esther A. Stevenson. Alabaster. COURTESY, SEATTLE ART MUSEUM

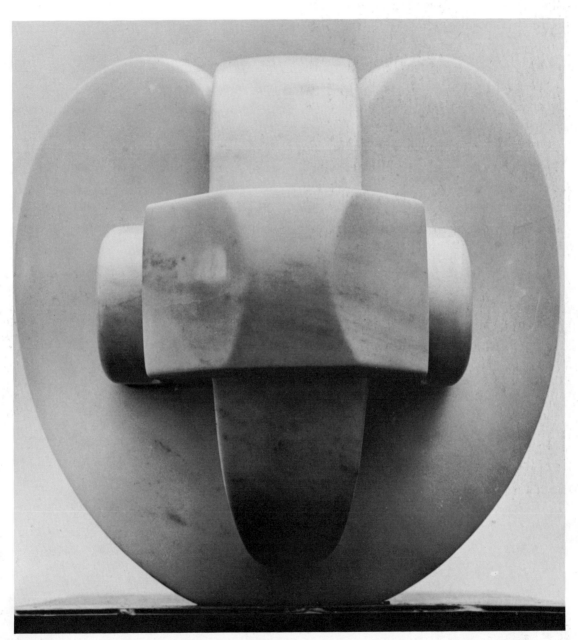

It's a Great Game, Andrea Cascella. White marble. COURTESY, BETTY PARSONS GALLERY, NEW YORK

Slate

Slate, a metamorphic rock, is clay and shale that have been compressed by the forces of nature. Slate, besides its use as blackboards, floors and roofing, is interesting material for the carver. The layers may tend to split, but with proper handling this problem is easily overcome. Work in the direction across the layer formation and use instruments sharp enough to penetrate the layers without splitting. Slate is quite soft. It may be etched with a nail or a hand motor tool; cut away with a keyhole saw or a hacksaw; textured with any sharp instrument such as a toothed chisel, awl or screwdriver that has been ground to one or more points.

Buy slate from stone companies, floor tile suppliers or slate quarries in Pennsylvania, Vermont, New York, Maine and Maryland. The stone, usually light to dark gray, is also found in brown, red and green.

Blackboard slate more than a quarter of an inch thick is suitable for relief carving. Slate slabs are most adaptable to relief designs, but if thick enough, may be worked into three-dimensional sculptures also. Slate is so durable that the writing on slate tombstones from the seventeenth century is still legible. The most noted slate piece is the "Palette of King Narmer" from about 3000 B.C. in Egypt.

Slate chunks often will suggest a design. You can trace a form, outline it in chalk on the slate, then scribe it with a sharp tool. For carving use any of the tools illustrated in previous chapters. Slate can be brought to a high luster by melting beeswax on the smoothed surface. (Melt by placing the wax under a sun lamp or in the sun.) Rub the wax in, buff with a soft cloth, then remove excess wax from the incised lines with a scriber. Slate pieces may be hung on a wall or mounted on a block, depending upon their shape, size and weight.

Darting into Fray, Boris Gilbertson. Slate. COURTESY, GALLERY A, TAOS, NEW MEXICO

Group of Four, Barbara Hepworth. Slate. COURTESY,
MARLBOROUGH FINE ART LTD., LONDON

Two Figures, Barbara Hepworth. Slate. COLLECTION,
THE TATE GALLERY, LONDON. COURTESY, MARLBOROUGH
FINE ART LTD., LONDON

Slate Churinga. Austria. Secret tablets believed to represent the soul of an individual. COURTESY, FIELD MUSEUM OF NATURAL HISTORY, CHICAGO

Palette of King Narmer. 3000 B.C. Slate. COURTESY, EGYPTIAN MUSEUM, CAIRO

Buffalo William, Boris Gilbertson. Slate. COURTESY, GALLERY A, TAOS, NEW MEXICO

Other Good Carving Stones

There are other kinds of metamorphic stone, not as popular as the marbles, but ideal for carving. These inexpensive and easy-to-work stones should be considered as both training material for the sculptor and as media for a finished sculpture. Always, the final form matters more than the material or the technique. Regardless of the beauty of a piece of marble, if the form is a cliché or unconvincing as an artistic statement, the piece is not a success. A valid form in stone less rich and colorful than marble is still a successful sculpture.

Soapstone has become more popular in recent years, thanks to the carvings of the Eskimos. American Indians and the ancient Chinese used it for ornaments, images and utensils. It is used in industry today and in a very powdery form for tailor's chalk. Higher density soapstone is excellent for carving. It is inexpensive, polishes to a high, rich luster, is easy to cut, and is relatively permanent.

Soapstone, also referred to as *talc* or *steatite*, is called this name because of its soapy or greasy feeling. Colors range from white through gray, to green and brown. The stone often contains small amounts of other minerals which give it a greenish tone and some unusual, surprising color variations.

Soapstone blocks are easily cut by sawing. Fine chisels, knives, dental tools, the motor tool and anything that will cut or carve may be used. Some soapstones do have grain, and experience helps determine where the grain is and how it should be handled.

Other stones in the examples that follow include African wonderstone, varieties of lava or featherock, pebbles that often defy classification, and gem stones.

Two Walrus. Eskimo carvings. Soapstone with ivory and bone. COURTESY, AMERICAS GALLERY, TAOS, NEW MEXICO

Woman and Skin, Koom of Povungnetuk. Soapstone.
COURTESY, NATIONAL FILM BOARD, CANADA

Woman, Kinasasi of Sugluk. Soapstone. COURTESY,
NATIONAL FILM BOARD, CANADA

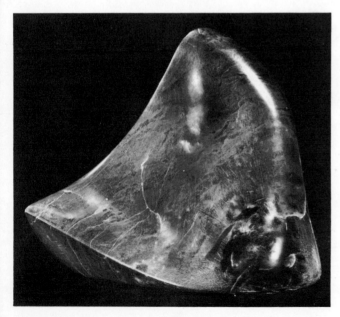

Abstract Form, Irene Riley. Sedro Wooley talc
(soapstone). COURTESY, SEATTLE ART MUSEUM

African wonderstone, like soapstone, is soft and easy to carve. It is a very compact variety of shale, composed of earth-clay substances, available in large blocks from sculpture material suppliers. Wonderstone polishes beautifully to a warm satiny finish.

Private Patios, Ruth Ingeborg Andris. African wonderstone on a black marble base. COLLECTION, MRS. HARRY SCHNEIDERMAN, CHICAGO

Proud Young Woman, Ruth Ingeborg Andris. African wonderstone.

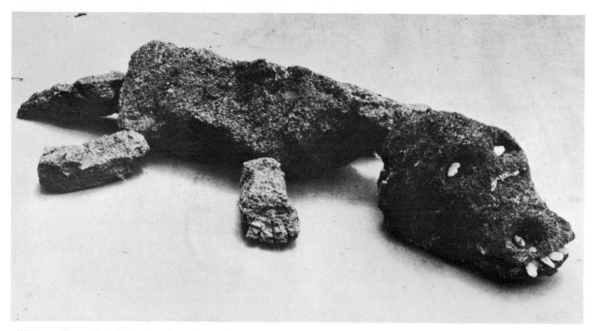

Alligator, Dona Meilach. Featherock or lava rock. A highly porous rock, easy to chip and carve, often used in Japanese gardens and for outdoor sculpture.

Featherock can be broken into odd shapes easily with a hammer and screwdriver. It is adaptable to large, bold shapes and can be carved with any sharp instrument and smoothed with rasps and files. Pieces can be assembled, as in "Alligator" above, to form a whole composition.

Rhythm Rock, Ralph Hartmann. This is a closer grained featherock than above and lighter in color. Because of its porosity, it is not necessary to polish; much of the beauty is in the natural texture.

Pebbles and Small Stones

Stone carving in miniature might be an apt description of the experience you get by working with pebbles. Pebbles or small stones have been formed in the same way as larger stones, except they have been broken off and subjected to many natural weather conditions. Pebbles may be as soft as soapstone or as hard as granite. They are often so beautifully shaped that they require little help from the artist other than imagination, slight carving, perhaps polishing and mounting.

A walk on the beach, along a river's edge or in a woods will yield an amazing variety of stones. Many exotic stones are available from garden supply dealers.

Test the softness of a stone with a nail. If it's scratchable, it is carvable with any of the tools shown throughout this book.

River Rock, F. Pierce. COURTESY, CRAFT HOUSE, ARROYO SECO, NEW MEXICO

Turtle, Marie Taylor. Long Island fieldstone. COURTESY, BETTY PARSONS GALLERY, NEW YORK

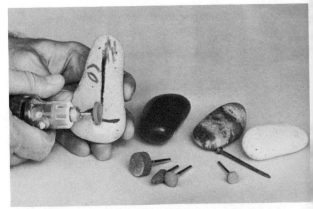

Oddly shaped pebbles can be given personalities by carving with the stone grinders of a hand motor tool. Notice the different shades and textures of the stones shown; they vary in hardness also.

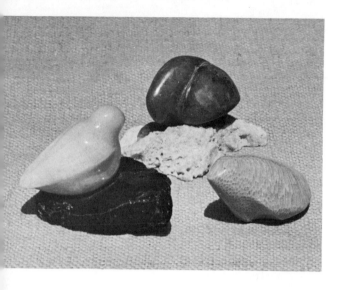

The stones suggested the forms which artist Abby Wadsworth worked with dental drills and burrs, then polished. Left to right: Honey onyx, rhodonite, Iowa Petoski.

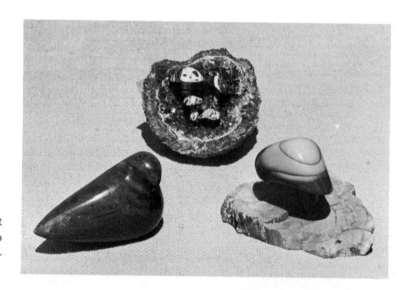

Stone shapes, Abby Wadsworth. Left to right: Mexican onyx bird, Pueblo onyx mushrooms, Jasper stone mushroom on petrified wood.

Tiny Buddha figures, each carved from jade, quartz, ivory, amethyst and others. COLLECTION, DR. JOEL D. ARNOLD, OAK PARK, ILLINOIS

Gem Stones

Certain minerals, called gem stones, have been broken off from large rocks and transported by water, often great distances; they sometimes become embedded in other rocks. Some fall into the category of semiprecious stones: jade, quartz, rhodonite, jasper, onyx and others. The stones vary in texture, color and density. The carving tools required depend on the stone, but most such stones are relatively soft and can be shaped with rasps, files and the hand motor tool. Often, the shape of the stone will suggest a form to carve; waste as little of the stone as possible. A book on gems will supply facts on identifying these various stones and describe their qualities.

Reclining Water Buffalo. Dark green jade. Ming Dynasty 1368-1644 A.D. COURTESY, ART INSTITUTE OF CHICAGO

Lantern with Carved Panels of Bird and Floral Decoration. Spinach jade. Ch'ing Dynasty 1644-1912. COURTESY, ART INSTITUTE OF CHICAGO

Pendant. Jade. Costa Rica. COURTESY, FIELD MUSEUM OF NATURAL HISTORY, CHICAGO

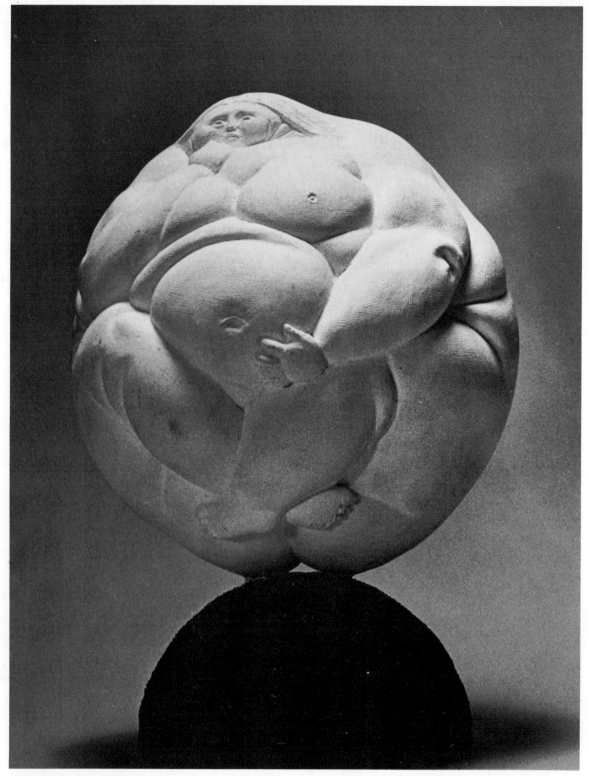

Spherical Figure, Eldon Danhausen. Hydrocal. COURTESY, ARTIST

6 Plaster and Other Dry Mixes

There are several dry powdered mixtures on the market that, when combined with water and allowed to harden, become as carvable as soft stone. Their advantages are many. They are easy to store in dry-mix form. They may be made into any size and shape, depending upon the container they are poured into to harden. Color may be added to the mixture or applied afterwards, and it adheres well. Blocks can be prepared as needed and are ideal for the hobbyist, artist and, particularly, for the classroom.

Forms made from powdered mixes may be carved while they are still slightly damp. Even after they are hardened they may be immersed in water and softened sufficiently to make carving easier.

Another advantage is that by pouring the mix, you can place objects within the block to create several effects. In the example shown on page 105 balloons were placed in a milk carton and then plaster was poured in. When the plaster was dry, the carton was peeled away and the balloons removed. Beautifully smooth negative round interior cavities resulted. An oil base clay, placed within the carton before pouring the mix, will also create odd shapes in the finished block. Adding real objects to the mix as it is poured provides textures and surprise areas when you begin to carve.

Mixes also allow you to create shapes that are as odd as the container. Try pouring plaster into a heavy rubber balloon. When the plaster is hardened and the balloon is peeled away, the plaster form has a smooth surface, ideal for additional carving. By placing rubber bands on a long narrow balloon before the plaster sets, a wild variety of shapes can result. The mix may also be put into a plastic bag and shaped with the hands as it hardens; then additional carving can be done to modify the form.

There are plasters and, dry-mix stone products available with different colors, textures, drying times and hardnesses. Plaster of Paris is most commonly known and available in hardware stores. Casting plaster, hydrocal, white art plaster and molding plaster have varying characteristics and should be investigated for art purposes. These materials usually dry more slowly than plaster of Paris and are less likely to chip after hardening. (They are especially good for classroom use since their slower drying time allows a teacher to mix a large batch and distribute it to students while it is still soft and workable.)

Art suppliers carry Crea-Stone, Whittle-Stone, Karva-Stone and other versatile sculpture media in dry-mix forms. Some of these are pre-colored in blue, red or gray. The resulting blocks so resemble stone that it is often difficult to tell one material from another.

When using any of the powder-mix products, follow instructions carefully for mixing, agitating to remove air bubbles and drying times. Because such products are water-base, it is best to use waxed, rubber or flexible plastic utensils for mixing and shaping. The dried block separates from a waxed container easily. If you use cardboard containers, wax them with a special

Always add plaster to the water a little at a time, mix, then agitate to remove air bubbles. With quick-drying plasters work quickly, because adding more plaster to a batch that is already partially dry will weaken the final block.

separating medium or vaseline to prevent the paper from adhering to the plaster.

Never pour waste plaster or the other powdered products down drains; they tend to harden and clog the drainage system. Work on waxed paper or newspaper. Be sure the waste materials harden, then throw them in waste containers.

Plaster and other powder-mix products can be carved with any or all of the tools shown throughout this book. In addition, there are plaster carving tools as shown on page 105. Always clean your tools after using them by removing dried plaster with a wire wheel or wire brush. (The water content of the mix tends to rust the tools.) A light coat of machine oil on the tool will prevent rusting.

For additional ideas for plaster, see *Creating with Plaster* by Dona Z. Meilach, in this series.

In addition to plaster, there are other dry-mix products with a variety of marvelous characteristics for use in classrooms and studios.

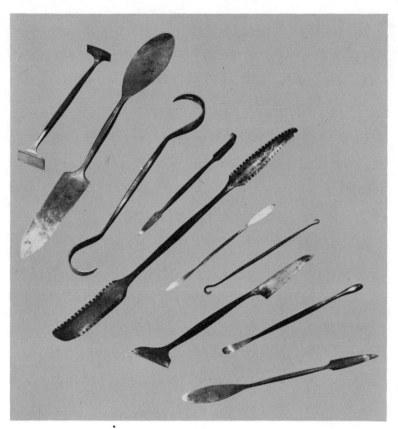

These special plaster carving tools have odd shapes that enable you to get into tiny, hard-to-reach areas, to add small details, to create unusual textures, and so on. Many are similar to stone carving tools, which may also be used for plasters.

Inflated balloons can be placed in a waxed milk carton, their stems taped to the outside of the carton and plaster poured in. When plaster is dry, the carton is stripped away, the balloons broken and removed. Smooth cavities result on the interior of the block. With additional carving a beautiful sculpture, like the one at the right by Harriet Arenson, can result.

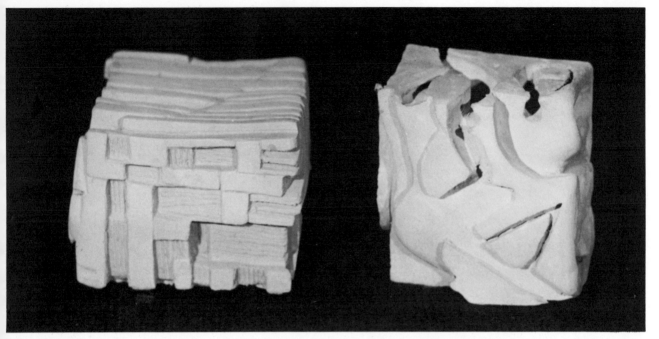

Plaster blocks by students of the Chicago School of Art and Design, Ltd. have different carved designs on all six surfaces that had to be carefully integrated.

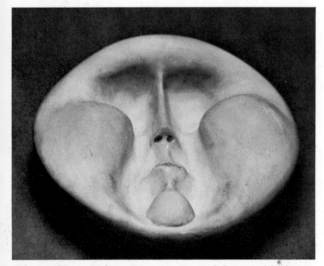

Plaster Face, Robert Pierron. Carved from a block poured into a carton, worked with Surform rasp, files, sandpaper and steel wool.

Curves, Josee Rauch

Plaster blocks can be intricately carved with narrow rasps and files; these by a student of the Chicago School of Art and Design, Ltd.

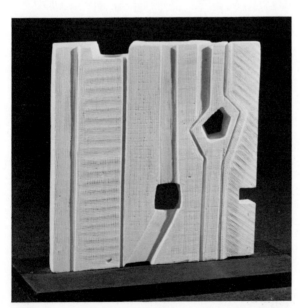

Design, Carl Sandquist. Plaster design.

Fish Forms, Student, University of Illinois, Champaign-Urbana

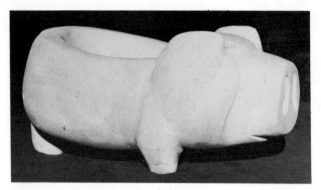

Pig, Bob Pemberton

Male Torso, Larry Pascoe

All examples on this page, by Ravenna High School students, Ravenna, Ohio, were carved from blocks made by pouring plaster into milk cartons. Some of the forms were painted and stained.

Hand Holding Ball, Tom Frees

Lion Head, Daryl Lussen

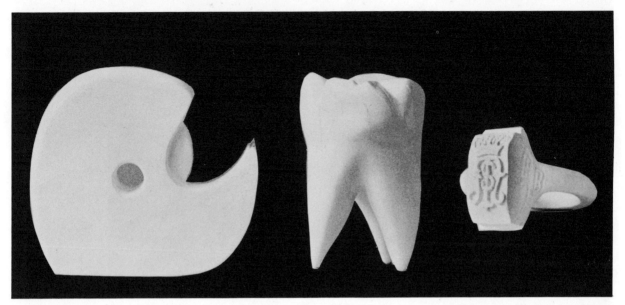

Student problem at the Institute of Design, I.I.T., Chicago, was to recreate well-known objects in plaster several times their ordinary size.

Study for the Pavillon de Flore, Jean Baptiste Carpeaux, 1865. In the nineteenth century plaster was mainly used as a study material, but today is often used as a finished work of art. COURTESY, ART INSTITUTE OF CHICAGO

Animals. Any of the dry-mix stone products may be given a coating of paste metallic products, spray paints, acrylics, stain and a variety of finishes. These figures have the appearance of bronze sculpture. COURTESY, ART-BRITE CHEMICAL CORP., NEW JERSEY

Two Heads, Sidney Dubin. Plaster covered with Model-Metal Bronze. COURTESY, ART-BRITE CHEMICAL CORP., NEW JERSEY

Sleepy Baby. Crea-Stone. Any toothed tool will create texture in this material. COURTESY, AMERICAN ART CLAY CO., INDIANAPOLIS

The Viking. Whittle-Stone. COURTESY, WHITTLE-STONE, COLORADO SPRINGS

All dry mixes can be easily carved with sharp knives and plaster tools.

Mother-in-law's Tongue. Whittle-Stone. COURTESY, WHITTLE-STONE, COLORADO SPRINGS

Winding Form. Whittle-Stone. COURTESY, WHITTLE-STONE, COLORADO SPRINGS

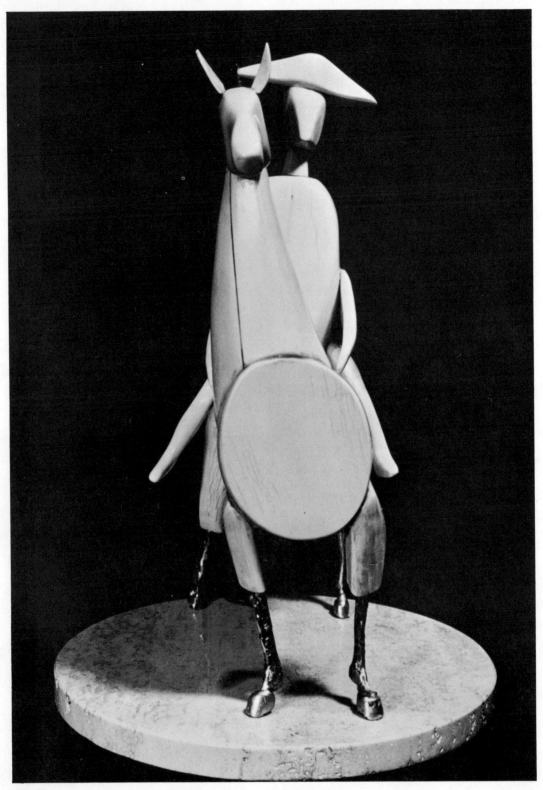

Carabiniere, John Kearney. Carved from one large elephant tusk, sterling silver legs and mane.
COURTESY, ARTIST

7 Ivory, Shell and Bone

The oldest carving materials used by man were bone, ivory, horn and shells—all from animals. Such carvings date from the Stone Age, and it seems reasonable that the carving tools used were other pieces of the same materials. Today, craftsmen use shell and bone primarily for jewelry, horn mainly for powder horns, and ivory for jewelry and statuary. With the exception of ivory, all are easily available, inexpensive and simple to work. In workability, their qualities are probably closest to the plastics.

The main reason for introducing these materials in this book is because they are available, yet often overlooked by the teacher and the artist as material for artistic expression. They are carved with the simplest tools shown—files, knives, small saws, drills and the hand motor tool.

Ivory

Ivory, an artistic medium for thousands of years, is found as statuettes and utilitarian items such as hair combs and jewelry. Today, small pieces of ivory are most often used for decorative handles on cutlery, for napkin holders and jewelry. Most of the ivory carvings come from the Far East (see the example on page 4).

Ivory is an organic material secured mainly from the tusks of elephants, walrus, hippopotami and some wild pigs; and also from teeth. The density of ivory differs depending upon origin. Generally, ivories take a high polish using a gentle abrasive with a soft dampened cloth. Ivories tend to mellow with age and change color. In high humidity they may warp and crack.

Shells

Seashells have such varied beauty that they are most often used just as they are as decorations. Yet putting your imagination to the carving of seashells can give some unusual results. Shells can be found along lakes and streams, or purchased from shell suppliers who advertise in craft and hobby magazines. Clam and conch shells have the largest surfaces for carving. Conch shells have such beauty and translucence that they are the prime material for carving cameos in the Italian jewelry industry. The layers of shells have unexpected color variations and are particularly good for relief and intaglio. Usually the rough outer layer is removed down to the white and pinkish layers.

Shells should be worked with very sharp knives, then soaked in olive oil, washed in soap and water and polished with a soft bristle brush.

Bone

Remove marrow and gelatinous tissue from bone before using to prevent rotting. Carve with any sharp instrument or file and and smooth with the blade of a knife. Use bones from meats, or ask your butcher for larger leg bones that may be carved, then assembled and painted. Bones have about the same chemical makeup as ivory, but are less dense. They vary in hardness. Bones should be dried thoroughly before applying any surface coloring.

Horn

Horn can be ordered from craft and gun supply houses (many are used for powder horns). Slaughterhouses often give them away or sell them very cheaply. Horn is best worked by first filing off the rough coating, then using a stone grinding wheel to remove layers quickly until horn is one-sixteenth of an inch thick and practically transparent. The thinner the horn, the more beautiful it is, because the pigments show in various layers.

Remove file marks by gently scraping the surface with a sharp pocketknife. Final carving may be done with a knife, the motor tool or the electric woodburning tool or pencil shown on page 52. Apply a polishing rouge to the horn and buff with a cloth covered wheel.

Shell Ornament, Maya Culture, 1300. COURTESY, ART INSTITUTE OF CHICAGO

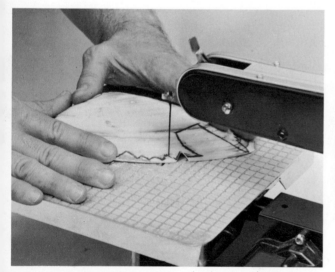

Large shells may be sketched out with a felt tip marker, then cut with a small band saw or a file.

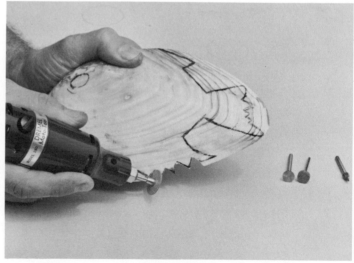

Edges can be smoothed, further shaped and even engraved with the cutting tips of the motor tool.

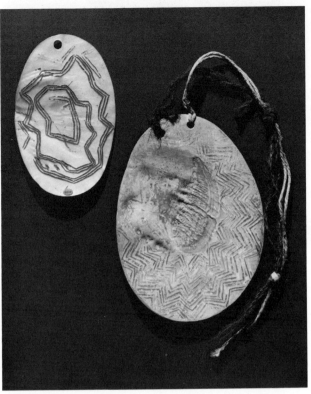

Shell Pendants, Australia. COURTESY, FIELD MUSEUM OF NATURAL HISTORY, CHICAGO

Rhinoceros horn carved with a row of animals, China, Ming Period. COURTESY, FIELD MUSEUM OF NATURAL HISTORY, CHICAGO

Eskimo Tools made of carved bone with metal blades. COLLECTION, DON BLAIR, TAOS, NEW MEXICO

Wild Boar, Robert Pierron. Carved cow vertebra with ball bearings for eyes.

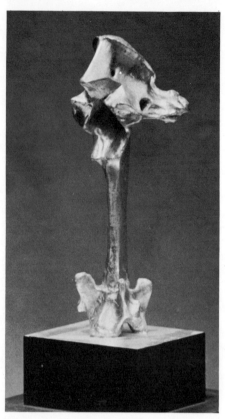

Fior D'Oro, Robert Ray. Carved cow bone with gold leaf. COURTESY, MISSION GALLERY, TAOS, NEW MEXICO

Etched ivory gaming tally. China, Ch'ing Period. COURTESY, FIELD MUSEUM OF NATURAL HISTORY, CHICAGO

Whale bone pato or stabbing club. New Zealand. COURTESY, FIELD MUSEUM OF NATURAL HISTORY, CHICAGO

Life Cycle, John Kearney. Ivory. COURTESY, ARTIST

Mother and Child, Eldon Danhausen. Ivory. COLLEC-
TION, SIDNEY KORSHAK, CHICAGO. COURTESY, ARTIST

Detail from a screen with carved figures of ivory and
bone. Taiwan, contemporary. COLLECTION, DR. AND
MRS. EARL ELMAN, CHICAGO

Index

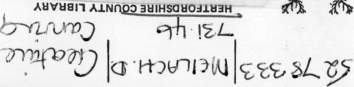